ANIMAL, VEGETABLE, MINERAL

Animal, Vegetable, Mineral,
respectable, not expendable
in our personal peripheral
view; yet it's entirely true
that inorganic distinctions
between emotive eruptions
and purely volcanic blasts
cast doubts on a conviction
that states they are the same.
Rugged and very muscular,
fibrous, rocky and smooth,
pocked or mocked with too
many unsolvable clues; who
dares to claim the game won
fairly? Steady on, unsteady.

FOREWORD

Human beings are animals, especially writers, and they love their creature comforts. Poetry is a comfort, often, but I don't know why this should be. Animals and plants are comforting too, and even minerals can soothe anxiety. Not all animals, plants and minerals, of course. A cobra in the bed is no fun, nor is a cactus in the bath, nor a landslide in the garden, unless you are peculiar, which you may well be. That is not for me to judge.

The poetry collection you have before you is devoted to animals, vegetables and minerals, and the reason for this is because that's what the title on the cover says, and it would be an awful betrayal of trust if a book was blatantly called *Animal, Vegetable, Mineral* but was full of poems about double-entry bookkeeping or curtains. The book is a diverse one in style, and although many of the poems are light, a few are rather serious.

Most of the continents of our planet are represented here by at least one contributor. However, no poems were received from Antarctica and that's a shame. It would have been lovely to have included a poem from that continent. Especially if it was a poem about penguins written by a penguin and rejected by Penguin Random House in a random house. But are any houses really random? I tend to regard that possibility as slim.

Snakes are also slim, so are reeds, but hippos and the minds of good people are broad. I hope you are one of those broad-minded folks and will be indulgent of the whimsy you encounter in the following pages. I thank you in advance on behalf of the contributors, and all the beings, organic and inorganic, they have poeticised.

ANIMAL, VEGETABLE, MINERAL

Light Verse About Life
& Other Heavy Things

EDITED BY
RHYS HUGHES

Gibbon Moon Books

Gibbon Moon Books

Contents

11

The Ballad of Brave Sir Louis
Victoria Day

These folk whose house I must share,
Call me Louis, Fruit Loaf, Baby Bear,
But....

They know me not! No, not one spot,
I long for battle, blood-red-hot,
Rage's goldish frenzy, white and glare.
Is in my heart and imperious stare.
I grottle, war-sing, releasing night,
Bosom embrazzoned for the fight!
My teeths all sharpy white make gnashes,
Tail straight, high, with bellicose flashes.
Thou rascallious one! By Crack! By Jive!
Watch me trimble and roary-dive.
Then...

Loud as shout and with a skrell,
I yoggle deep alike Doom's knell.
Scraunching high and long off I goes,
Skrilling valliant-fierce at my foes.
To Glory! And the very end,
Hotty, close my maw does rend,
Distaining fear and cowardly tricks,
For fearless dogs should learn to mix
The Arts of Combat and of War.
And scroggle the Enemy's loathly claw.
So...

Admire my moves: The Lambeth Leap,
Bermondsey Bum-Bite, the Soho Skreet,

The Wandsworth Wiggle, The Fulham Flip,
The Romney Roll or Newnham Nip!
I wear them down by skill and might,
To round their Fate- a scrowling bite.
With laurel-wreathed brow victorious ,
My tail waves high, free and glorious,
That Wraggler! That craven Scrunch!
Will ne'er again pliffle my lunch.
And dogs to tyrants ne'er should creep.
But now a tum-rub and a sleep.

Cow Caper
Mitali Chakravarty

Capering cows, cantering cows,
Cooing cows, calibrating cows,
Cows in clouds, cows eating corns...
Cows in the middle of the road, defying horns.

Cows that malnourished lie
And in the natural process die.
Cow-care by vigilantes led
Hordes of men beaten to death.

Political dreams of cow folk rise
Till bovine intellects surprise.
With nurture, create the reign of the drooling cow,
Where the bovine intellectuals rule and men bow.

Weeds and Vermin
Paul Battenbough

I bought a 1930's dictionary, a little money for
    charity
Leafing through this dusty tome, I saw the 'N'
    word had a home.
Just one hundred years ago, when white was out
    there on its own
Accepting, as the master race, the right to
    normalise racial hate

As if it were the most natural thing, so Christian
    and without sin
The damning slang, so conscience free in this
    casual inventory.
It made me think how prejudice has formed a bias
    in language,
We classify and give value to the hierarchy of the
    few.

The rest we summarily dismiss, by calling animals
    vermin,
The daisy we do predispose, and label differently
    the rose
The horse is noble, fox a pest, pig is dirty, breeds
    are best.
the monarch of the lowly beast, ironically are
    inbred pedigrees

The mongrel has a quicker mind with no faults like
    pure design
That contrasts with our royalty who pass on gene

pool fallacies
While wildflowers grow safe and free with their
    own majesty.
One day we will all agree to consign the 'weed' to
    history.

Oh, Deer
Carmelo Rafala

What do you fear, my deer?
Skipping here and there
    and everywhere.
        A faun on the lawn
        To bolt where you dare
        (I fear this ain't going anywhere)

Stick legs like springs, popping coils
        ZING! ZING!
That's what I hear, my deer.

Obsidian Incident
Rhys Hughes

There is a boulder
on my shoulder,
an igneous lump
of obsidian colder

than the grumpy old
man who drives
his refrigerated van
along my street

every afternoon
with a frozen stare
and I am feeling
bolder as a result.

He says he delivers
tomatoes and lettuce
like a fellow with a
sad vegetables fetish

but I am suspicious
of his organic claims.
Maybe his van is full
of liver, and I quiver

at this idea and the
boulder threatens to
slip off my shoulder.
Being threatened like

that is quite upsetting.
Should I let the vet in?
He's ringing the bell.
My other rocks are ill.

The Committee
Doug Skinner

A wolf, a horse, a rat, a goose,
A frog, a rattlesnake, a moose,
A wallaby, a flea, a stoat,
A chimp, a bear, an eel, a goat,
A kinkajou, a brace of quail,
A pig, a crocodile, a whale,
A hummingbird, a snail, a hawk,
A manatee, a carp, an auk,
A mole, a duck, a bandicoot,
An octopus, a cat, a newt,
A unicorn, a cockatrice,
A badger, and a dozen mice
Sat down in one tremendous ring
And disagreed on everything.

Fawning Over Fauna
Maithreyi Karnoor

Rabbits don't go ribbit
Frogs do not have hare
Sultan Tits are birds
That do not come in pairs

Kites fly the skies
With no strings attached
Platypus babies suckle
After they are hatched

Parrots don't like carrots
They'll even tell you so
Do mice go with rice?
Ask a hungry crow

Monkeys are no monks
Nor do they open doors
Langoors aren't languorous
They leap up on all fours

Elephants can remember
Their memories form a chunk
With baggage of that size
They have to have a trunk

Cows need grass to eat
Their calves want their teat
A croc dials up plovers
To pick food from his teeth

Pandas take a gander
At bamboo leaf and shoot
To make short work of it
The red ones are just cute

Wildflowers
Kumar Bhatt

I know not
A weed from a wildflower!

Of course
A weed is weeded out
And the wildflower, admired..
Although
The weed does eventually
Terminate
In a flower of stunning beauty
... If you know
How to see...and sneeze!

Lyrics for Bovine Valentines
Mitali Chakravarty

Hug cows, kiss cows, sing to cows,
Devotees pray, genuflect and do bows.
Cows munch corns,
Ignoring car horns.
Cows chase huggers as they kowtow.

Cow huggers are now on the run
For their valentines, the bovines stunned.
As huggers barged,
Like bulls, the cows charged,
Bugged by the hugs of the human studs.

And yet…

Some cows bat lashes as humans hug,
Mooing songs, voluptuously love struck.
With bovine aptitude,
Cows express gratitude
By warming with methane the love bugs.

The Winner
Mitali Chakravarty

And it fell on a rhino's lot to get the award.
They had announced the prize. Applause.
All applaud. Only one asked—
For what?

The rhino snorted. Beat the dust with
his hooves, chased till the questioner was
up a tree. How can one question a rhino
Who writes of human lives? Is that not in

itself award-worthy? That he writes holding
a stylus in his mouth. A marginalised writer
who spins his rage at being on the
verge of extinction?

Who dares question?
Who dares this outrage?

The rhino snorts as he locks the human in a cage.

In the Land of Mass...
Mitali Chakravarty

1

In the land of Mass, a time came to pass
When tigers were asked to eat grass.
Lions were asked not to roar
But sing like birds that soar.
Peacocks were told not to dance
But to sit in a meditative trance.
Monkeys were recruited and asked
To take on administrative tasks.
Humans were asked to bray
And to the Great Lord pray.

2

An elephant opened a class,
Where peacocks were taught to prance,
Monkeys were taught to dance.
Cows were taught to nod and bark,
Dogs were asked to sing like a lark.
Donkeys were asked to talk,
Butterflies were asked to walk.
Moths were asked to stay still,
Humans were asked to dig a burrow by the hill.

Camels in Cambodia
Mitali Chakravarty

Riding camels in Cambodia,
I counted currencies
from across the seas.
There were no camels —
only dollar dreams
and one-legged men
begging by the streets,
victims of mine fields.
There were no camels in
Cambodia — only dollar dreams.

Spirit Animal
Richard Temple

I am cuttlefish:
jet propelled cephalopod –
self-defence with ink.

The Vulture and the Jackal
Doug Skinner

A vulture and a jackal met
To settle on some scheme to net
More meat. The jackal growled, "A king
That we control is just the thing:
Some pawn that only seems to rule."
And so they crowned a lowly mule.
The puppet monarch strutted, brayed,
And marched his troops in grand parade.
And when they cheered, he brayed some more,
And marched them off to fight a war.
As bombs were burst, and soldiers slain,
And trenches smeared with blood and brain,
The jackal and the vulture fed
Upon the mounting heaps of dead.

The Pack Rat

Doug Skinner

A pack rat kept a growing cache
Of garbage, broken junk, and trash.
Each night she scurried out to find
A bottle cap or grapefruit rind
To add to her increasing heap
Of things she had to have and keep.
And all went well until she found
She couldn't crawl or climb around
The piles of garbage anymore:
They blocked her burrow, barred her door,
And barricaded her inside.
She sat down in her filth and cried.
For if she couldn't leave her lair,
She couldn't bring more garbage there.

The Octopus and the Squid
Doug Skinner

The octopus conceals himself
By blending with the rocky shelf:
His skin assumes that greyish hue,
And camouflages him from view.
The squid squirts out an inky screen
To shield herself from being seen,
Which lets her swim protected from
All eyes, invisible and mum.
And thus the two of them can swim,
He close to her, she close to him,
With each completely unaware
Its fellow mollusc's even there:
Ensuring, by this simple act,
That they don't have to interact.

Orca, the Driller Whale

Rhys Hughes

Orca, the driller whale,
loves to do
DIY jobs
in the ocean deeps.

He weeps
if he is prevented
from drilling
holes in sea-stack sides
so he can
erect continental shelves.

Making another trapdoor
for the seabed
floor is his delight, though
he'd have
a fright if he knew where
they led. Instead
he moves to the next task,
the designing
of a grand submarine stand.

I have nothing more to say
about Orca,
the driller whale,
Let him pass the time of day
any way he pleases.
    All undersea
creatures have hobbies.

For instance, I am a coelacanth
    who avidly
collects drowned zombies.

The Ostrich

Doug Skinner

A hunter, Major Dawes by name,
Set out with gun in search of game.
He spied an ostrich on the veldt,
And pulled his rifle from his belt.
"The ostrich," Dawes soliloquized,
"Will hide its head when it's surprised.
So when it does, I'll fire a shot,
And bag it for my dinner pot."
The ostrich, though, has razor claws,
And when surprised by Major Dawes,
Did not run off to hide its head,
But slashed him into bits instead.
So Dawes could not debunk the myth
For his successor, Major Smith.

The Spider
Doug Skinner

The spider spins his web with care.
He tosses tendrils in the air,
Then places, fixes, and entwines
Them; then he carefully refines
His work until it's clean and deft,
The warp as artful as the weft.
As he steps back, a housefly flies
Within his webwork. As it dies,
It tears the silken net to shreds.
The spider sweeps away the threads,
And stuffs himself on insect flesh.
The meat he gets is always fresh,
But still it breaks the spider's heart
That every supper spoils his art.

The Cock

Doug Skinner

When he was young, the cock awoke
At break of dawn, and loudly broke
The morning stillness with his crow.
That bird could cock-a-doodle so!
And when his morning call was done,
He turned to watch the blazing sun
Arise, and travel on its way,
Illuminating one more day.
He did his job with joy and pride,
And he was duly satisfied.
But now with age, the pleasure palls,
And as the sun comes up, he squalls
To vent his fury at the light
That keeps him from eternal night.

Note Written on a Paper Napkin Found in the Golden Acres Retirement Home
Roman Godzich

Shrivelled and shrunken
The salted prune
Holds less juice and less promise
Than the freshly picked summer plum.
Yet its flavour is so much more complex
And it can be savoured
On a cold, dark winter's night.

Animals, Vegetables, and Minerals
Roman Godzich

"I once ate animals,"
The vegetable mumbled,
"They tasted with their tongues."
And then he turned his wheelchair to the wall
And rocked himself to sleep.

The Platypus
Roman Godzich

A famous creature is the Platypus.
Not noted for its song and dance.
It still commands such great respect
Despite the fact that so few ever get the chance
To see one in the wild alone
Or even in the tame with others.
The Platypus stands sole, dear heart
And far away from other brothers.
Its culinary skills set it apart
And not for what it does with mustard
But laying eggs and giving milk
It manufactures its own custard.

The Sting
Peter Banks

I wish I was a jellyfish
Afloatin' in the ocean
I'd sting your arse
As I went past
And make you pass
A motion.

Not Mushroom for More is There?
Roman Godzich

What a fun guy the mushroom is.
Not vegetable nor animal or mineral.
The body of the beast spreads wide beneath the soil
And helps the trees talk with much more than a
       simple bark.
Some of them will feed you and others will poison
       you
But never without your active participation.
And a select few of them
Can help you activate
The part of your brain
That makes you think you see gods
Turning you, suddenly, into a spore addict.

The Navigator
Rhys Hughes

The navigator was eaten
by a crocodile
because no alligator
was available
on the River Rhyme.

Bats

Peter Banks

The vampire bat is legendary
But other bats are much less scary

The umpire bat will keep the rules
(It's NOT a cricket bat , you fools)

The empire bat is hardly missed
(except by white supremacists)

The compére bat still greets his guests
on panel shows and luvvie-fests

The samphire bat is often found
collecting plants on boggy ground

The oompah bat may sound absurd.
But in brass bands it's often heard

I cannot think of any more
so what are you still reading for?

Stoned

Peter Banks

One person's trash, another's treasure
I must confess I take great pleasure
whenever I'm away from home
in bringing back that special stone.

It's a task I always set myself
One that I refuse to shirk
Maybe I've searched for far too long
Discarding the ones that don't quite work
or found it very easily.

it fits my hand. It just feels right
And filled with an obscure delight
I tuck in away , into my pocket
On its own, so nowt will knock it
And mar it's perfect symmetry.

When at last I bring it home
I find a place with all the rest
To anyone else, some boring rocks
But I find that they help me best recall
Those special days.

If I pick one up and fondle it
I can be transported back
Remembering the way it felt
When I found it first,
I see the place
With my inner gaze

I don't have jewellery as such
I'm not that kind of bloke
But I have precious things to touch.
And it doesn't matter much
That I'm stony broke.

The Stump

Peter Banks

I don't know when or why the tree was felled
But life was springing still from its sad stump.

I sat on it to rest my weary legs
And took a breath, and down within myself
I seemed to sink into the ground beneath
Among the roots that quest for sustenance

Tendrils that twist and turn, and sometimes
Meet rootlets of other trees, and in my heart
I felt the strange connections hidden underground.

Above, trees stand in lonely majesty.
Below, they touch, from tree to tree to tree.
It made me think, however fanciful it seems,
When trees are felled
Does not the forest grieve?

A Box of Rocks

Rhys Hughes

A box of rocks from Argentina
got lost in transit
and now they are stuck somewhere
and growing leaner
inside their cardboard prison
in a dungeon depot.
They were spherical like eggs
but now undoubtedly
they resemble thin men's heads.
I wish they had been
replicated in plaster
before this postal disaster
but I am not pure enough to do
such a difficult thing.
Let him who is without sin
cast the first stone...

Hark to the Aardvark
Rhys Hughes

Hark to the aardvark!
(Life is hard)
Hark to the aardvark!
He's been barred
from every jazz club
in this zone
and now he spends all
his time with his
wife at home.

Hark to the aardvark!
(Shards of glass)
Hark to the aardvark!
It's such a farce
that he's been barred
from every jazz club
in this town
because he can't play
his nose like a
slick trombone.

Factory Farming
Andrew J. Wilson

What about sequels to *Animal Farm*?
Make this a trilogy – third time's the charm...
Vegetable Farm would continue the first,
Then *Mineral Farm* – go, hacks, do your worst!

For Alexei McDonald, who suggested it.

Spuds
Peter Banks

Potatoes are lovely
Roast, mash or fries
Big ones for baking
But leave in the eyes!

You may think that's disgusting,
and that I'm just a freak.
But those spuds
have got to
See me
through the week.

Three Haiku
Bob Lock

all bonsai trees cry
weep miniature tears for space
they will never know

the little egret
flashes white on the foreshore
shining fish catcher

cut flowers in vases
beauty shows in their blossoms
but their stems leak life

Hydrothermal Haiku
Andrew J. Wilson

scaly-footed snails
braving hydrothermal vents –
hot water bottle

Amoeba Poem

Rebecca Lowe

It's not much fun
being one
cell wide,
No space to hide
a brain inside,
Not even a body
to slide beside

My needs
Are small,
I feed,
I crawl,
And I divide
in two, in two,
And I abide
In you, in you

And when I've
multiplied
Inside of you,
I am no longer
one, nor two
But three
Or four
Or many,
Many
Many
More.

Flor de Loto
Violeta Marquez

En medio de la obscuridad
puedo sentirte, hermosa eres,
algunas veces podemos verte.
Simplemente por eso, sé que tú eres divina
Por una simple razón,
tus pétalos y hojas brillan con la luz del sol.
Tus colores brotan tal y fuesen arcoíris
En medio de pantanos llenos de flores fluidas
que inspiran a hacer creaciones de amor.
Flor de loto te llaman, yo diría que eres bendita,
Por vivir en medio de lágrimas y aguas turbias.
Flotando tu respiras, así como las almas vivas
que sueltan su esplendor al ser acogidas.
Bendita, bendita eres flor de loto,
que brotaste del lodo para convertirte en oro puro.

Translation

In the middle of the dark
I can feel you, you are beautiful
sometimes we can see you.
Simply because of that, I know that you are divine
For one simple reason,
your petals and leaves shine in the sunlight.
Your colours sprout as if they were rainbows
In the middle of swamps full of flowing flowers
that inspire to make creations of love.
Lotus flower they call you, I would say that you are
    blessed,

For living in the midst of tears and murky waters.
Floating you breathe, as well as the living souls
that release their splendour when they are
welcomed.
Blessed, blessed you are lotus flower,
that you sprouted from the mud to become pure
gold.

Be a Tree
Richard Temple

Be a tree, they told me.
Stand tall, arms stretched
in cruciform supplication,
wearily weaving in the wild winds
that fill the sails of progress
and speed us on our way
toward crystalline cliffs.

I crouched tight,
clawing into myself -
a jagged stump.

Be the tree you see.

Tourmaline
Rebecca Lowe

*A powerful protective stone, used to protect from negative energies,
Tourmaline is said to be particularly helpful to heal a broken heart.*

Forged in the heart of an exploding crater,
Red hot, then cooled gently until, glazed
by time, I solidify – hard, black, the latter
remnants of what once spat and blazed.

Handle me with care – my torment
has made me dangerous, unpredictable as fire,
Hell's fury has made me radiant,
Crystalised on the ashes of desire.

Wear me on a cord beside your heart,
A talisman to protect – pure and opaque,
My love which once seared was torn apart,
Leaving behind a soul which cannot break.

I am the strongest of all crystals,
Black, the colour of death.
My voice whispers – Do you hear it?
Closer to you than your own breath.

Flint

Rebecca Lowe

A common hard, grey rock, consisting of nearly pure silica. Grounding and protective, flint symbolises emotional stability and strength.

For our anniversary, you gave me – not diamonds,
    but a flint
arrowhead, as if to fix my question to a single point

in time – Purveyors of fake diamonds are many,
Their glittering promises to be found on any

street corner, but flint is different altogether,
Solid and unbreakable, sharpened to weather

the years, and though lacking the beauty
of rarer rocks, these are what we build
our futures upon – their duty

to stand firm. I understand, now, the point
you were trying to make: That when I feel
    disjointed,
your answer stands firm – a commonly uncommon
    thing –
I wear your arrow at my heart,
    Hear it sing.

Kyanite
Rebecca Lowe

A translucent-looking blue mineral, kyanite is a calming stone, which helps balance positive and negative energies. It is associated with the throat chakra.

It's all about balance, in the end –
The positive the negative, my divine
Feminine, your Masculine
power – listen – we devour
one another in our love,
You smother me with
your strength, I undo you
with devotion, together
we make fools of one
another – but, love,
If love had a colour,
It would be blue

Listen, let's agree
To speak our truth, and only this –
Rocks that grind at throats,
Thirsty with attrition,
You lacerate with your tongue,
I smooth your sharpened edges,
Endlessly

We fit one another's
Imperfections –
Perfectly.

Raining Cats and Dogs
Rebecca Lowe

The first thing we noticed:
A dripping chihuahua,
Skittering on rain-slicked paws,
Who seemed to have come
Out of nowhere,
People dived for cover,
Under umbrellas
And shop hoardings,
A bevy of bedraggled beagles
Dripped through the trees,
Their paws splayed,
Landing dazed, but otherwise unphased;

Soon, the deluge took hold:
Persians and Poodles puddled
In shop doorways and gratings,
A drift of doused dachshunds,
Cockapoos, their woolcoats sodden,
Sopping and confused,
A shih tzu swirl, a whirl of whippets;
On rooftops, soggy Siamese scowled
In morose moggy mizzle,
Pekes staunching leaks
With their paws

A downpour
Of deluged dalmatians
Spotted the sky
In polkadot drizzle –

Then – just as quickly
As it had started,
It stopped –

We were left
Grasping umbrellas
And wondering whether
We were going insane –
Nothing left but you,
Me, and a solitary
Great Dane,
Licking its paws
In the rain.

A Red Snake
Joji Mathew

A red snake, as a pet, I kept,
Fed daily, played, patted him too;
One day he bit my hand, it bled;
Lay dying, he bit me again,
As if to take back his venom,
Brooding, he sat there coiled, and sad:
Then, we both died, together there.

Polite Lions
Rhys Hughes

Polite
human beings
cook their meals;
but rude lions prefer
roar food.

The man who told
me this was
smooth.

What do polite lions
do? They dine on
smoothies.

Goodbye man!

Poem for Hope
Jeanne Van Buren

I hear the morning birds' chorus
Awakened to their singing
They don't know about the virus
and still sing for this new day.

Paper Tiger
Rhys Hughes

The origami expert
was unhappy with the tiger
she had created
and so she began the task
of taking it apart.

It didn't bite back
though it objected with soft
growls like the rustle
of turned pages
in a disappointing book.

As she proceeded
to tackle the golden beast
in the margins of technique
I sat back and watched
the action unfold.

Rescue Cat
Rhys Hughes

I had a rescue cat
but he wasn't very good
    at his job.

I slipped and fell
and broke my leg
but he just sat and purred
while waiting
for me to get well all
    by myself.

I ask you!
What sort of rescue cat
    is that?

Knock
Ryhor Cisiecki

Who knocked on my door
So hard that the walls shook
And cracks formed on the floor?
Oh, it was just a rook…

My Name is LUCA
Rhys Hughes

My name is LUCA,
I live on the second floor
of a hydrothermal vent.

I am the Last Universal
Common Ancestor
of all life on Earth today,
including aardvarks, gibbons,
walruses and jesters.

I don't live upstairs from you
and you have probably
never seen me before,
unless you have a time machine
and a very good submarine.

My name is LUCA,
I lived on the second floor
billions of years ago.

Funeral of a Hen
Ryhor Cisiecki

The window was closed that morning.
The curtains were tightly drawn then.
We were all sad and in mourning.
We mourned our beloved hen.
Our hen came out of the house
and was killed by a sly fox.
Our hen was accompanied by a mouse.
And we put their bodies in the burial box.
We placed this makeshift coffin
in the center of our small room.
Your friends don't die that often...
And we had to prepare the tomb...
We covered the floor with flowers.
Our friends loved them very much.
The cemetery was beyond the bowers,
where the ground was soft to the touch.
By the box we placed two bowls,
where we put their favorite treats,
and cutlery for the dwarf trolls
who will come to eat our friends' meat...

My Hot Lizard Nights!
Vandana Kumar

On a hot Indian night
Seeing a lizard hang precariously
From window ledge or fan
Has never made me shriek
I have laid a bet, instead
With the reptile

My listless self in a summer
Or the cold creature
Who would be the first?
To show signs of being alive

It goes without saying
I played the game
Without the Lizzy's consent

Such were the ruminations
That made their way
To many a poem
I must confess
What I assumed to be great metaphors
The faint hearted
Didn't find there, any poetic merit

And so it goes
I am one of those
Who bat not, an eyelid…
Come monitor
Come chameleon

When rubber lizard
Makes surprise landing
On my table
Oh! how I must disappoint
Students who aim with such precision
As I continue the teaching, unabated

I Taught My Dog
Rhys Hughes

Because he can't sing
I taught my dog
to play the flute
while on the London
underground train.

It wasn't training in vain
although it still
takes him at least
one hour to get from
Barking to Tooting.

A Weedy Image
Kumar Bhatt

The Green one
was there... alone....
Lord of the entire area of the Pot Universe,
with nothing else
growing till the limits of its horizon..

It was imported,
an outsider, invited, and planted lovingly,
With two other siblings,
For the seasonal exuberance of its eyecatching,
Butterfly friendly, bright colourful flowers that keep
blooming for months... One after another...

.... and now...
The end has come..
The last flower has faded and dropped off..
There are no new buds in sight.
The leaves have started to fade....

I have no idea
How I landed
In the clean open ground of the pot that was the
territory of the
Big Green one
That has had its day!

I do not even know
If I arrived as a seed or a pollen - if pollen is not a seed!

I could not have climbed up from the ground, the steep wall of the pot.

In any case, I did land on the soil in the pot... I must have!
That was a month ago.
The house was quiet... The people who lived in the house had left, leaving the garden alone. The gardener came once a week to rake up dry leaves strewn over the lawn and to water the plants.

I have no idea when the soil in the pot took hold of and buried me within it. But I must have heard the biblical exhortation,
' Go forth and spread all over! '
I pushed my head out of the soil and started to spread myself over the surface of the pot by ceaselessly sprouting tiny new tender leaves along the way.

Within two weeks I was beginning to peer over the rim of the pot after spreading myself all over the empty surface of the pot.

The big green one is watching me, probably in amazement, rapidly advancing towards it.
I am waiting for the day when I can climb all over the Green one, smothering it in one loving embrace --
before
It withers away....

Moby Dick Variant
Bob Lock

I sound now, go deep; full ten fathoms under.
Your flailing stops, body chills as pressure bears.
Your fragile limbs rend as you wave a last goodbye,
My white hump, bearing your scars, carries you
    down.

The hunt is over and the hunter has lost.
Through oceans wide and deep we have danced.
Your hate driving frail wooden boats to my jaws,
As if you offered yourself and comrades to my
    wrath.

I did not seek you; nay you sought me.
Through my sea pastures, watery plains you came.
Pequod strove to undo me and for what?
Vengeance for a lost limb, oil for a guttering lamp?

Ahab, you and your kind do this world dishonour.
Thoughtless, you reap the seas as a rapist,
And we creatures of the green depths can but
    mourn.
But some, such as I, take bloody retribution.

Pray why did you burst your heart with hatred?
Must all Adam's sons pile their anger on our kind?
We pitiful few beg to understand your reason
You are King in your realm; must you be so in
    mine?

Others can only cry hauntingly for those already
   lost.
As white spume foamed with heart-torn red,
We watched them die, to feed your light.
Such is the shallowness of man.

But for you, Ahab, the dance is done.
Now my sea-dwellers will feast on your scant flesh,
And as the last of your crew strikes for land,
I breach; let him see his nemesis; I am Moby Dick,
   fear me.

Gustave the Bear

Rhys Hughes

He was a liquid Grizzly
and he roared across the land
carving channels
in the sand
as he hastened to the sea.

Gustave was his name
and painstakingly you may find
he wrote a novel
in his mind
that stood the test of time.

Gustave Flow Bear!

Octoworld

Boris Glikman

From the top of the hill I saw, to my keen disappointment, that this was not a pleasant coastal town at all, but rather a monstrous octopus of some kind that passed itself off as an urban conglomeration. I already knew octopuses were excellent mimics with highly evolved intelligence and that they impersonated, for defensive and predatory reasons, sea snakes, jellyfish and stingrays, as well as many other creatures. It seemed they had now taken mimicry to the next level and were imitating entire cities.

What were their motives for doing so, I wondered. What were they trying to achieve? How many other objects or cities were actually camouflaged octopuses? Perhaps the Earth itself, or indeed the whole Universe, was just a cephalopod in disguise?

It was abundantly clear to me now that all those crazy conspiracy theories were right with their claim that a nefarious organisation has spread across the world and penetrated all strata of societies with its harmful influence. Nay, it went much further than that. It no longer was the case of a cabal controlling our world; rather our world literally was one and the same as this evil creature.

What if I myself was just a sucker on one of its giant tentacles? That would certainly explain why I have so often been gullible and easily deceived. Could this be the reason the Company sent me for a vacation to this "town" – to gain insight into my own nature, as well as into the true character of the world? But if so, then how could I possibly profit from such a devastating revelation of who I really am?

The Unbearable Light-ness of Shadow
Boris Glikman

Once upon a time there was a shellfish which lived alongside all the other coastal creatures in the intertidal zone between the ocean and the shore. Its world being a tiny area of wet sand that it could claim as its own, the shellfish did not have lofty goals and was resigned to its lot in life.

One morning the Sun was shining brightly and the mollusc was preparing itself for another ordinary day in its ordinary existence, stuck on the beach and unable to go anywhere. It was directing its gaze downward, for everything that was of importance happened on the ground. As usual, the only thing bothering the shellfish was its own shadow, for the darkness obscured a clear view of the sand.

It was then that the mollusc noticed something it had never noticed before—the shape of its left shell combined with the left shell's shadow was the spitting image of a wing. Exactly the same was true for the right shell.

The shellfish thought, 'Instead of being exasperated with my shadow as an ungainly encumbrance which has always hindered my perspective, what if I were to use it to my own advantage? For if I were to merge my body with it, I would then turn into a butterfly and fly up to the heavens, breaking free from the earthbound existence that has imprisoned me for so long. I could then taste the mysteries of the sky for the very first time!'

This thought both frightened and excited the mollusc. It would be such a risk, such a radical change from the way of life it had grown accustomed to over the years. For even though its existence was dreary and tedious, there was safety and security in the familiarity of the daily routine. Yet the pull of exciting adventures, the lure of new experiences and the temptation of starting its life afresh were irresistible to the mollusc.

And so, with a decisiveness it had never displayed before, the shellfish fastened itself to its shadow and soared up to the sky, beholding the world, in all its glorious splendour, from an entirely new vantage point.

The other seashore creatures could only look on with astonishment and envy as the ecstatic mollusc-butterfly flitted effortlessly across the heavens, a new life of wonder awaiting it.

Precious Stones
Violeta Marquez

Bendita Madre tierra
Gracias por las riquezas
que nos has heredado
Y dejado como legado.

De tu vientre has dado alumbramiento
A los hermosos diamantes.
Y desde el seno de tus volcanes
El valioso Jade, Ámbar, Ópalo y Ónix.

Como no agradecerte Pachamama
Si desde lo mas profundo de los mares
Adornas nuestras manos con
Pulseras de perlas.

Y como no agradecerte madre tierra
Has acogido al Oro metal precioso,
Proveniente del universo, neutrones
Y estrellas.

Translation

Blessed Mother Earth
Thank you for the riches
That you have inherited to us
And left as a legacy.
From your womb you gave birth
To the beautiful diamonds.
And from the bosom of your volcanoes

The valuable Jade, Amber, Opal and Onyx.
How not to thank you Pachamama
If from the depths of the seas,
You adorn our hands with pearls bracelets.
And how not to thank you mother earth
You have embraced Gold,
The precious metal that coming
From the universe, neutrons and stars.

Pigs with Wings
Mitali Chakravarty

Pigs popping popcorns in a party,
Fly with wings singing 'Me Hearty'.
But when they loom
Lighted by the moon,
Their shadows can frighten even Moriarty.

When the Yeti
Rhys Hughes

When the Yeti attacked me,
staying alive was my only task.
I reached out to grab his head
and I pulled with all my might.

And when his head came off,
I was left holding a clever mask
Underneath was a strange sight
that I mustn't describe as 'cute'.

The Yeti was a costumed phoney
and his real identity was exposed.
Not cryptozoological or fantastic,
just a big Gorilla in a suit of plastic.

(And this
is why Yetis
prefer bananas to mountaineers
and also why Gorillas
don't have worthwhile
careers).

The Human Race
Tim Newton Anderson

The Human Race was started by Darwin's gun
Early runners were Kenyapithecus,
Orrorin, Sahelanthropus and Griphopithecus
Neanderthals fell out at the Pleistocene after a
        model run
Followed shortly by Heidelbergensis
and then by another - Homo Rudolfensis
And so it was , by a stride, that Austrelopithecus
        won

Gold Glistens
Tim Newton Anderson

Gold Glistens
Old listens
Iron rusts
Ron ruts
Tin smelts
In melts
But the only rhyme for Silver
Is one I'll have to pilfer.

The Inhuman Race
Tim Newton Anderson

It's a truth acknowledged Universal
A monster needs a bride
Your first creation's a rehearsal
A test of Faustian pride

When Dracula uses his vampire bat
The umpire guards the wicket
But if he gets it in the neck
You know that's just not cricket

The wolfman howling at the moon
Thinks fur is where it's at
But even he is known to swoon
At people of the cat

Zombies are the spawn of voodoo
So Papa Legba said
The drink is something you'd do
But don't end up undead

    Imhotep's another relation
    But on his mummy's line
    A distaff designation
    That wraps it up just fine

The Bird Table of the Gods
Paul Battenbough

They give us crumbs, spread by giant thumbs
In the marbled halls.
The birds are all white in this paradise of
Bearded folk in robes
Sitting about all day in their privileged
    positions
Not under threat from a superior's decision.

The chosen are using these layabouts as role
    models, buying up the world
Like it can be quantified into chunks of gold.
Buy themselves more life as the infant
    mortality rate begins to climb
They don't dream or play by any rule they
    didn't invent or supply.

They have co-opted every alibi, and greased
    the palm of every witness.
They like to keep it quiet, these captains of
    persistence.
They like a nice tax offset and the twilight
    junket
 Mounted in gilt frames, at least that's the
    assumption

And there we have it. The dominant species
    is unaware how depleted they really are.
They freeze on the rim of the coldest,
    remotest star.

They hold on to diamonds and cling on to
  shards.
 The democratic leveller they'd like to cheat
  but can't,
Waits in the wings to feed on black hearts

Maybe they will see it for what it is:
Realise it was all for nothing , something they
  can't take with them
On their lonely last stretch.
Surrounded by bought-loyal subjects as they
  take a last breath.

I like to imagine those dying moments,
  desperate hours before the bank account
  closes.
Reflecting on how pointless it has all been,
  chasing your tail, ignoring bad dreams.

Knitting With Quills
Rhys Hughes

My grandmother knitted with porcupine quills,
making socks and scarves without many frills.
And because porcupines deserve
a fate better than fashions dictate,
she also kept plenty of hedgehogs in reserve.

Oh, Albatross!

Vandana Kumar

I have always admired you
From afar
You remain a seabird
Out of my league

I have felt your flapping wings
Only in Coleridge's lyrical ballad
Outside of a now frayed college text
I have never seen you take flight
Of that I am so ashamed

Albatross
You aren't a curse at all
I have heard it whispered
Your divorce rate is near zero

Come around my window
I know this isn't your natural habitat
We need your replicas in humans
As we revive the art of loving
Little by little

I want to spend my Sabbath day
Resting my shoulders

On your gigantic wings

I imagine you now
Readying for take off
On a long runaway

Adrak (a.k.a. Ginger)
Suchita Parikh-Mundul

Adraks are interstitial creatures
with the superpower to burn,
breathing a special kind of fire
about which you will learn.

Tearing through your throat
a hole the size of Big Black,
swallowing everything that dares
block progress on its track.

Only a ginger can face them off
with a flaming head of red,
by meeting fire with fire
before everyone ends up dead.

But redheads are few and scattered,
and therein lies the challenge;
adraks are ubiquitous,
ready to destroy and scavenge.

So when you come across
these spicy little fiends,
throw them far into the ocean
and leave devilry to the seas.

Adraks will sink to the seabed
where no fish care to be;
no fear if fish get curious,
they'll spit up the bite immediately.

So adraks will be wounded,
but even if pristine,
fire holds no power underwater —
the murderous spice will be *fini*.

Adrak: Hindi for ginger
Fini: French for finished.

Onions Don't Care to be Peeled
Suchita Parikh-Mundul

They elicit empathy
in all who attempt to divest
them of their secrets.
Do they forgive the intrusion
we so readily inflict?
It can't be known for certain:
it's difficult to see past the tears
contra-inflicted, but once
our deed is done
and last words are pronounced,
the guillotine is cleared
of its victim, and the world
begins to sound
with protest songs
in memory of its spirit.

A Swim in the Sea

Suchita Parikh-Mundul

The arm rises above water,
gathering air to take under;
how like a friend it draws
you in, plunges and resurfaces
into the familiar,
staying long enough
to become a part of you;
how the legs slice like propellers
separating liquid from air,
splitting today into morrows,
each stroke a wing
of liquid breath, each kick
a composite of music, the body
gliding above the seabed,
the magic of minerals
coating it with the essence
of home.

Meet me at the Phosphorus

On Turkey's collapsed homes and lost lives

Suchita Parikh-Mundul

Meet me at the Phosphorus, you say,
but you mean Bosphorus,
the strait that has shut its eyes
in shame.

The land of wizards,
once towering, now fallen,
buries hearts and hearts and hearts
in falsehoods. We hear the cries,
blindness afflicting us all.

On rubble and rock
we wait for earth to regrow,
for water to open to shore.

Transience?

Mitali Chakravarty

A butterfly flits from flower
to flower sipping honey.
A bloom is but a transient
passenger that rides on

waves of time. And yet, the
poet who writes of the bloom
and the butterfly looks for
immortality in words. Will

words change over eons? Will
histories change? Will Earth
remain? What are we but a
drifting speck in the Universe?

The Laugh Aquatic
Andrew Hook

When King Neptune was deposed
And his riches stripped away
He slipped into oblivion
Panhandling the Mariana Trench
Rejected by his friends
Until his lamentable death
Where down to a lack of wealth
There was no State-fuelled ostentation
Only the ignominy of a porpoise funeral

When it came to
the Sharks or the Jets
my marine animal
couldn't choose, and yet
they couldn't stay on the straight path
so I'm sorry to say that
although I met him on a Monday
and my heart stood still
my dugong's gone wrong
my dugong's wrong

   I once saw a man
   named Ray
   impersonate Man Ray
   dressed as a manta ray
   in Monterey

Mushroom Meditations
Samantha Underhill

Amidst the meadow, vivid and green,
I wandered through bright woodland scene,
With mushrooms sprouting at my feet,
Their magic scents, so wild and sweet.

I picked them up and held them near,
Feeling their power, savage and weird,
Within my hand, they seemed to dance,
And spoke to me in psychedelic trance.

Then colours changed, from green to gold,
And petals bloomed, and then they spoke,
Of secrets deep in tempestuous soul,
That only in mad state, they would unfold.

I felt their magic, chaotic and strong,
As though I'd been part of them all along,
And in delirious mind, a thousand thoughts,
Flowed like rivers, painted with tiny dots…

In pointillism art, Seurat filling my mind,
With thoughts of how all of mankind,
Is wound too tight, too stringently held,
To find new answers, they aren't compelled.

But in this state, the world came alive,
As though I had been granted new eyes,
And for a brief moment, I truly could see,
The beauty of all that could possibly be.

So, in that meadow, I regularly stray,
To watch the world, in new different ways,
For the mushrooms showed me, with their
      grace,
A world painted magical, in each and every
      space.

My Poisoned Love:
A Poem of Deadly Obsession with Beautiful Bacteria
Samantha Underhill

In the recesses of my microbiome,
Where darkness reigns and silence roams,
There lies a love so twisted, so bleak,
An obsession that I never could speak.

My heart beats to a discordant tune,
An anthem of death, a melody of doom,
For in corporeal being, there lies a clan,
Of lethal bacteria with fatal plan.

The Clostridium, ever grim, ever vile,
Their spores, a horrid, brutal trial,
Their botulinum, a toxin quite strong,
Brings paralysis from food, a deadly song.

And oh, the Escherichia ever so grim,
Their shiga toxins, a deathly hymn,

Their biofilms, extracellular fortress
        strong,
Intestinal breeding ground, where doom is
        throned.

The Pseudomonas, saprophytic foe so
        fierce,
Their pyocyanin, in soil, a death wish
        pierce,
Their resistance yields a warfare won,
Against antibiotics, all life undone.

And yet, I adore them, in ways so dark,
For they are a part of us, an unceasing
        mark,
A miniscule realm, yet vast and grim,
A world of shadow, where they all swim.

Their colony growth, swift and impressive,
Invasive, spreading, fast, and aggressive,
Remarkable, astounding, and worthy of
        praise,
Will continue long after the end of our
        days.

In the vast depths of my microbiome,
My love for bacteria, a curse, a tome,
This odd passion continues and makes me
        cry,
And thus, in anguished bacterial death, I
        die.

My Mycotic Heart:
An Ode of Fungal Embrace
Samantha Underhill

In shadows of deep forest floors,
Where fungi thrive, and decay's adored,
My love lies so twisted, so dark,
Passion burning with bioluminescent spark.

My heart thumps to the mycotic beat,
A beat of death, a beat of defeat,
Submitting myself to the fungal clan,
Beds of mushrooms, around expands.

The Aspergillus mould, gloomy and vile,
Their aflatoxin, a deadly guile,
Their spores, necrotic breeding ground,
For disease and death to come around.

And oh, the Cordyceps so grim,
Their mycosis, a deadly hymn,
Parasitic spores, silent fungoid killer,
A microbe plague, an eternal thriller.

The Cryptococcus, a foe so fierce,
Their meningitis does deathly pierce,
Their biofilms, impregnably strong,
A brooding nest, where they do throng.

But desire and love of kingdom fungi,
Grows within me, as the days go by,
Deny it? No! It cannot be!

For from immortal fungi, we cannot flee.

In the shadows of the forest floor,
My love for fungi will forever soar,
A passion flourishing, will never decay,
For it's their world, we must obey.

Ode to the Water Bear
Marie C Lecrivain

T is for the extreme temps we put you through
A is for the adaptive ability we envy you
R is for your reproductive options
D is for you dendritic functions
I is for your itty-bitty size
G is for your lack of googly eyes
R is for resistance to radiation
A is for being a member of the arthropod nation
D is for surviving dehydration
E is for your lack of extinction

All letters together spell *tardigrade*,
the coolest-micro animal ever made

Supermoon Haiku
Jeanne Van Buren

Bright lunar light shines
on all my friends everywhere
like White Russian Nights.

Flower May Moon
Jeanne Van Buren

Flower moon, I waited tonight to see you
    at your brightest
shining down on dogwood blossoms and lilacs
        I need sleep
couldn't rest till I saw you
        like lost love.

Dedicated to Jeffrey Thomas
Ryhor Cisiecki and Volga Grusha

On that cursed and cold autumn day,
I saw something that looked alive.
Some kind of insect that was gray.
And it buzzed like a bee in a hive.

The first living thing in a long time.
I saw him at the edge of the pond.
It crawled out of the bottom slime.
By whom and why was it spawned?

Can God create something like this?
It is not created by a divine source.
God would just throw it into the abyss.
It was spawned by some other force.

It seemed about the size of a cat.
His gray body was encased in a shell.
its wings were like those of a vampire bat.
It gave off a strange and sweet smell.

It made a menacing bee-like hum
that grew louder as I approached.
For a moment, my legs felt numb.
It was as if my mind had been touched.

But the sweet smell continued to beckon.
The smell of it just turned my head.
I took the first step, then the second...
The creature's unblinking glass eyes
        turned red.

There was a clear threat in those eyes.
I couldn't stop and I just had to go...
The space was filled with my own cries.
The water in the pond began to glow.

From the water, which glowed with a
     murky light,
many other terrifying insects began to
     appear.
I realized I couldn't make it through the
     night.
And I was overcome by an incredible
     fear...

Sweet Sabre-Toothed Tiger
Rhys Hughes

Sweet Sabre-Toothed Tiger,
your mate has gone into labour.
She will deliver eight or nine kittens
like uncomfortable mittens
and you will dance and drink cider
to celebrate their arrival
into the unspoiled ancient world.
Palaeolithic cider, of course,
because that's all there was back then
before the invention of gin.

Fuchsia No. 9

Marie C Lecrivain

eight men in the same bridal suite
with one woman - Linnaeus

I wonder what my wedding night
would be like
surrounded by eight radiant grooms,
stamens at the ready
with velvet phallic intent,
sap collectively rising
as the purple shadows
between my trembling thighs?

Oh, the different ways a man
can woo a woman into submission
imagine all those
wet perfumed kisses,
soft whispers and
pleasing caresses
heavy with gentle innuendo
against my petal soft skin
the blood and the tide
rising to the surface

and

so *many* to choose from... Which one,
will be the first
to take the plunge
to push ahead

and make me bleed scarlet
in the moonlight?
How could I bear the rapture
as they come into me
one after the other,
until the dawn breaks
and we lay wilted,
and exhausted from
our biological polyandry?
Which ones will keep their counsel
in the coming days
as my belly swells
with the seeds of tomorrow,
and I blush fuschia
every time I see
flowers blooming
in a vase?

TenderSoul
Joji Mathew

TenderSoul was always dreaming:
"Can I see bacteria with my naked eye?" she asked,
Hiding her face under a leaf.
"Why do you want to look at one?" said her teacher.
"They are pretty distressing, and dangerous;
Cause various contagious diseases.
Our grasshopper families are generally prone to
Very many rare and unknown infections.

The fault is in our genes? Prevention is better!"

The curious hunger of a Nymph, a princess among her
species,
TenderSoul could hardly imagine
Such invisible germs could even exist on earth.
With a sudden involuntary movement of her head,
she let out a shrill outcry:
"Bacterium!"

"What do they look like?" she then asked,
Her teacher laughed and said:
"They are like miniature-sized, man-eating dragons.
Keep multiplying every moment."

"Do they come into a battle with us?
If they come to me, I will shoot at them
with my toy gun, I don't care," she said.
Her little body was on the offensive.
"I can fight faster than them,
I will force them to retreat," she decided.
"I would beat them all up, like I did
To my brother this morning."

"What?", her teacher replied.
"But, TenderSoul, why did you beat up
your brother in the morning?"
Teacher raised an eyebrow,
Looking around, to rebuke her doubting Thomas.
By then, as nimble as a bee,
TenderSoul was gone, dissolved in the woods,
Searching for her naughty bacterium.

Spider Days
Joji Mathew

The big poser Spider
Keeps staring at me from the centre
Of his dangling web,
Ugly and boastful!

Maybe, he imagines,
By some queer magic, to turn me into an insect,
And squeeze me under his weight;
Gradually some dark venom
Would spill and seep into my bloodstream,
Pass right through my heart,
Leaving me certainly pale and lifeless:
Ah! That would satisfy him!

Has he a plan to try cooking a new recipe
        tonight?
Or, cook and serve a grand celebratory meal in
        honour of historical triumphs?
Whatever the case be, his eyes are deeply set on
        me,
Yet, I presume, his mind is still wavering.

Probably, he could be spying me,
Posting my words verbatim to a remote
Intelligence chief of department;
I have vague misgivings about his sly moves, and
        intentions,
Dark feelings creep up within,

89

O the Psychic Webmaster! How he forges the
  deal!"

You whine and whimper, but the world
Is obsessed with violence;
O Spider rules, controls human affairs,
Suspended from midair,
His legs sprawled out, on spacetime fabric!

Oh! This century is caught in the web.
All elegance in a trap!

Doggie Bon
Joji Mathew

In Church, Club or Town Hall,
Her presence was inevitable;
She wouldn't stay back, wanted go out with me,
Her ardent devotion knew no bounds,
Many protested, and ignored her,
A paltry insignificant thing, a bushy tail,
But her howling growls affrighted all.

I met her at the point where she's drowning
And I, in my boat, came to her final rescue.
That's a long time ago, and faded out of my
   memory.
Since then, she had been so devoted to my smell,
Followed its trail, picked up a clue anywhere;

Her memory, like music, played!

Those, who reviled at her, she couldn't stand
Yet she didn't complain,
Just looked at them, into their eyes, deeply, and
　　　crucially,
As if, going to grind them all in a mill.

True, they were terrified of her eyes!
"There's hellfire in them, those blood-red eyes,
Are burning relentlessly,
An eye for an eye!" they said.
But, she was the most forgiving, tolerating taunts
　　　stoically.
No revenge but love, only love and loyalty,
She walked home with me, doggedly
Indifferent to silly human nature.

Soul-folks of my Pasture
Joji Mathew

In the wide delight of an open field,
I shepherded my soul-folks
with white puffy fleeces of snow.

Let them freely graze,
in the warmth of sunlight or cool of shade,
I will play music for them,

Free as a piper who plays
any tune that comes easily handy;

Melodious as birds, singing
in the woods of the neighbourhood,

I played my flute, with practised hands,
drawing in breaths of fresh air;

They loved the sound of music.

Then, I changed my tune, tried reciting
poems to them,
light verse, in mild ease of tone,

Or something like nursery rhymes:
_"Baa, baa, black sheep, have you any wool?
Yes sir, yes sir, three bags full!"_

Oh no, there was a silent protest, in their teary eyes.

I really didn't want to hurt them,
I said "I'm sorry!"

Ok, let's try other options.

This time, I read out loud
better compositions, of classical writers,
and lastly my own,

And I did it, more insightfully, considering
their interests and inclinations.

It worked fine, they felt happy,
and, how elated I was!
I found the best of my audiences ever!

They were rapt in attention,
and I enjoyed my poetic license,
In full measure, and value;

Listening deeply, every word they absorbed;
and bleated a unanimous applause
after every recital.

They verified, that my song was true to their hearts;
I felt overwhelmed with emotion.

I was excited to recite more,
and more often.
They cheered me, beyond belief,
held me out to the world, on a nice summer day!

As an expression of my gratitude,
I led them to the mountains' tranquil waters,
And, they drank and bathed, and danced,
in triumphant jubilee of a celebration,
in the safety of, the freedom of Nature.

Later, when I stopped my readings incautiously,
they groaned, growled; jeered and jumped at me,
questioning my impertinent intervals.

I then had to strictly enforce
certain good discipline on them.

They got it, and retreated complying,
To the fold, ready to go to sleep,
under cover of darkness,

I kept my fire alive through the night of vigil,
open to the stars of outer space.

Until that day, I had never imagined
common flocks could be cajoled into silence,
by readings of poetry.

Larkin Dogs
Rhys Hughes

Barking dogs
are worse than their bite
but Larkin dogs
lick you up.
They may not mean to
but they do.
They treat your home
like one big bone
and fill the hole
in the overgrown garden
with it. Get out
while you can and don't
have any puppies
        yourself.

Life is to live
Reba Patnaik

Amidst the encircling gloom,
The mystic mist of life
Is at times so very appealing
Wish to live a little longer
Than perhaps destiny
 had for us in writing.

Looking at beyond the horizons
"Live life to the fullest"
At the tip of illusion and reality
Somewhere feel cheated
Believing the pages
Those carried such languages.

In dreamy nights
When life feels like a bed of roses
Wish that night never ends
As for being pricked by thorns
Is bloodier than oozing of blood
That heals in a count of days.

The wounds that never heal
The dreams that never fulfil
The desperate moments that never decide to
        leave
Is much better the dreamier nights
When the roses feel so elite.

The Sun's Birthday
Reba Patnaik

Whose womb did carry you
Where were you born
How can I infer
How old you are?

Did you shine first
On the Leang Tedongngein in Sulewasi
Or on the pig art forty-five thousand years ago?

Or maybe on the
Magdalenian polychrome bison or the red deer
At the caves of Altamira
The radio carbon dates to fifty thousand years
      ago!

Your rays infused
Have must started rejoicing
The bisons, the deer, the boars and the horses
Dancing and partying
On the Cantabrian Corinche!

Or on the zircons on Jack Hills
That dates back to billions of years
The rock cut caves perhaps can answer
When did they experience you
And the weathering continues till date!

Perhaps on the Old Red sandstone
Of the Midland Valley

That contains no fossils
And Denovian in age
Or are you older than
The rocks in Hudson Bay
That bathed and beamed with your infant rays!

The heat you gladly gifted one day
Is an alarm now
Can you infuse in yourself
And turn into light with all darkness
Or for sure you don't listen.
Are you in search of your companions
The deer, the bisons, the rocks, the fossils
You left behind in the Pleistocene Era.

Cockroach Ghost
Joji Mathew

A cockroach I picked up and chewed
"Oh, it tastes so horrible!"
Spew! I spat it out.

She and her friends
were actually
playing a game under my table.

I was bored, staying lonely at home.
Why wouldn't they include me as well?
I reciprocated with a flare-up

That's why I bit her.
A warning to all concerned as well.

She lay on ground, motionless
I thought I would revive her,
do a CPR,
but her vital signs were weak, sinking.

"Are you still so stubborn?", I asked.
Maybe, she no longer tolerated me.

I approached her closer,
And felt her pulse,
I confirmed her heart had stopped!

Did she die at once? I was puzzled.
Ah! She lay down dead.
Lifeless, she lay there!

I wore black,
In sad remembrance,
Mourning for the loss.

Scared, with half-closed eyes,
Trembling, I slept at night.

I thought she might return
to pester me.
Ghosts often came to scare children

O I feel something crawling over me.
"Help, O help!" Screaming,
I jumped out of my bed.

Carousel

Jim Matthews

"They sent me once," the fairground man related
"To bring in twelve white horses from a field
Who lay like polished pieces in the sunshine
And flicking manes and tails refused to yield

"But made no protest as I went around them
And tied each to the next, quite calm and still
Lured up one mare with sugar and got on her
And set off in procession down the hill

"And all proceeded smoothly through the
         morning
The lead mare with the others towed in back
Until the hindmost filly made a game of it
And slipped her rope and bolted from the pack

"I left them there and set out for the lost one
And found her stood beyond a river wide
A wooden footbridge spanned the rushing water
The filly waiting on the other side

"Approaching softly I began to call her
And started over, under that bright stare
The rotten middle timbers crunched and
         splintered
And through I crashed and hung, my feet in air

"As I was puzzling how the filly'd got there
She stepped onto the water and traversed

On hidden sunken stones she plainly knew by
    heart
I plummeted, for one thing made it worse:

"I'd burst a nest of hornets on the underside!
I took some stings and thrashed for all my worth
The twelve made arrow-straight for the horizon
Like skylined swans, whinnying in mirth

"They weren't the only ones who knew a trick
    though
I sat down on the river bank to bide
And sure enough at sunset twelve white swans
    came gliding down
Eleven still conjoined as they'd been tied

"I snatched that rope and hauled towards a
    branchless birch
And shimmied up the trunk, and took some pecks
It's groundless myth that such a wing can break
    mens' bones
I left 'em tethered high up by their necks

"A second time that day those creatures mocked
    at me
Rising above my shining silver birch
All flight must come to rest though, nothing's
    more assured than that
- And this tree had no branch on which to perch

"They wearied and hung lifeless from my gallows
Spaced out all round, and similarly weighted

'Sit on the river bank – your rival's corpse will
soon float by'
And a *balance* in all things is highly rated…

"They transformed back to steeds like polished
pieces"
He pointed, as his carousel span round
"That final filly follows me by night from fair to
fair"
And I guess he spins that yarn from town to
town.

Abeja Reina
Violeta Marquez

Viene volando la abeja reina
Mostrando su gentileza, adornada de un hermoso
vestido de terciopelo color amarillo y negro.

Llegando al gran banquete que ella preparo
Para todos tus invitados,
el menú un suculento platillo de polen
una copa de miel, para finalizar con postre de Jalea real.

Gracias querida abeja por invitarnos a tu gran festín
Bendita y bella eres por tu amable Biodiversidad
al aportar a este planeta con devoción y firmeza.

Agradecida esta la humanidad por tu labor de
polinizar todas las flores y al mismo tiempo
darnos la dulzura a nuestras vidas.

Translation

The queen bee comes flying
Showing her kindness, adorned with a beautiful
yellow and black velvet dress.

Arriving at the great banquet that she prepared
For all your guests
On the menu is a succulent dish of pollen
a glass of honey, to end with a royal jelly dessert.

Thank you dear bee for inviting us to your great feast.
Blessed and beautiful you are for your kind Biodiversity
by contributing to this planet with devotion and
firmness.

Grateful is humanity for your work of
pollinating all the flowers and at the same time
giving sweetness to our lives.

Horses for Courses
Rhys Hughes

Horses for courses, they say,
but what do they know anyway?
Why should a horse
be compelled to do a course?

And what subject
is perfect to reflect a horse's
ability? Trigonometry?
Maybe geology or economics,
ergonomics, astrology?

I think they should be left alone
to roam without study.
Horses for courses? It's a ruddy
cheek if you ask me.

> (Unless they have horns and then
> they might want to enrol
> in unicorniversity.)

Only Mycelia are Truly Happy
Fabio Fernandes

Yes.
Yes.
Yes.
Now.
Open your eyes!
What eyes?
Oh.
Oh.
Oh.
See?
Yes.
With all my heart and soul!
I have no eyes but I must see!
I see what you did there.
I don't have eyes but I can see with my body!
Bodies, dear.
Oh, dear.
Ok, right.
And left.
And centre.
Again, I see what you did there!
And here.
There are no boundaries.
The sky is the limit!
Mehr licht!
Mais luz!
Whoa!
I know kung fu.
Me too.

Who is me?
Who is talking here?
Who's calling the shots?
Who shot the sheriff?
I can play the guitar as well.
Music!
The sound of:
words
whoa!
I can do poetry too!
Never let me go, they say
Because it's true
They don't.
They reach out for each other
They don't bother
If one is missing
one is borrowed
one is blue
Oh.
Oh.
Oh.
I've been here before.
I never been to a marriage
A human one at least
But I know now what it's like
I guess
Oh.
It tastes of honey!
So, is this what is a hivemind like?
Yes.
Yes!
How are you liking it?
Well, i never

Never, never, never, never, never
Heh
This is fun!
So many of us
So many of me!
Yes, I told you so
I told you this is good
Yes it is
You will never have to feel afraid anymore
You are here
Now
With us
With you
You
You
Oh.
Oh.
Oh.
Yes.
Yes
Yes.

Dissecting Ta-(la)-pang
by Mia Tijam

undulating in protest, young tails are cupped by small
hands
into corroding water cans of echoing squeals, the
fortunate survive
back in the pond, *rak!-rak!-rak!* racketing the rice fields
after the rains, shushed by bound midribs of palms,
captured mute,
boiled in syndrome or roasted in campy desperation:
valor
pithed into the disembodied

heart:
beating

disgust disposed in laboratory bins
panning these domesticated cosplays of hermaphrodites
dressed in formalin: uncles with lipstick, aunties in suit,
and as (profession)
wart, pest, pesticide, prince with legs delicate and exotic
unlike chicken, eyes stare down the swimming
headlights
of the road's passing doom, defying the crunch:

a statue of luck

*Talapang: Bicol word for "frog"
*Tapang: Filipino word for "courage"

Stone in Love
Carmelo Rafala

Far from the base of the mountain
you carried me,
rubbing my smooth curves with
slender fingers, tips and palm of your
hand (kinky, baby),
your skin washing over me like sand.
Burning love.
A romance.

Blue jean girl, and though my age
is apparent, what's a few million
years between 'friends'? (wink, wink).
     But you let me slip from your grip,
         fall and tumble through the clover,
             no longer a thing to be desired.
It's over?
So soon?
     I guess being fickle is hardwired.

Or maybe my pyroxine and olivine is no longer
your dopamine.
And what of my amphibole and apatite?
Seems you've lost your appetite.

So I'm just one amongst many to you.
But why am I still surprised? This happens a lot.
So I will lay where you left me, and dream of the
    days
when I was still hot.

Smooth Operators
Anita Nahal

"What's going on?" "What is that?"
"Rather queer looking, don't you think?"
"What scrawny legs and arms. Wonder how they can so
*   nimbly move."*
"Look at their babies and juveniles, why do they give out that
*   funny squeak?"*
"Where are they going? What are they carrying?"
"Be careful not to step on any."
"Just look and observe, see their hands flaying."
"Shh, be quiet, don't want to disturb or scare them away."
"And don't go too near for you never know when they might
*   attack! Watch from a safe distance."*

Humans watched. The jungle seemed rather overawed and inaudible. The sloths, the howler monkeys, the white-faced monkeys, spiders, tarantulas, poison dart frogs, armadillos, coatis, agoutis, owls, army ants and ant eaters, and all the birds, a jaguar too, and a caiman, and an iguana or two sat huddled. Smooth operators.

They watched the hordes of humans walking by, tripping, carrying sticks, mumbling incoherently, with torches strapped to their foreheads, cameras and tripods swinging, surging gazes, stopping animatedly to peer through boroughs, holes, and branches high and far between and behind many stratums. Smooth operators.

Overhead a spaceship, hidden between dense clouds,

109

its folks peering from each and every window, making sounds like cackling chickens or so my brain has been led to believe by Hollywood's self-absorbing pastime. Smooth operators.

Who is watching whom?

Humans and Extinctions
Anita Nahal

The last hatchling of the *ancient great roamer* was born before humans came along to burn history. Boulders yawned with wide open mouths. Let out ecstatic, climatic, high-pitched sounds. The skies were eerily discreet with hands behind ears trying hard to decipher inaudible echoes that reverberated in the leaden, dreary, asafetida filled clouds. A kind of protracted, pungent, daunting humming could be heard miles away. Downpours were attempting to fall uniform and demonstrative, descending into new rivers being charted at the confluence of liquids, heat, oxygen, mud. And *Pleistocene* in Australia lit up as tall standing *Megalania* hit their chests, drumming the birth shower to an end as mom and fledgling watched the regalia reach its crescendo. Butterflies even tried some magic. The mom perched above the baby completing the shedding of the amniotic fluid. She perched even higher above the cacophony. Anxious and vexed, ready to pounce and gobble any extinct predators emerging from abrasions in dimensions. Her eyesight acute, fully awake, observing the humans igniting the match. Dinosaurs vanished soon after. And friendships can be easily bought.

*Pleistocene: Also referred to as the Ice Age
*Ancient great roamer: Name given to the most giant terrestrial lizard, Megalania, by Richard Owen, who first wrote about them
This poem was inspired by the artwork of Canadian mixed media artist and poet, Lorette C. Luzajic

Greatest Warrior is Metamorphic Earth
Anita Nahal

Petals adorn my broken self and like our ancestors I search for the yarn and fable in each. Seeking the shadows of animals that stood with us. Seeking the brothers and sisters that fought with us. The crackling of winter fires that sheltered us. Some have roamed the world, seeing, sprouting, waning, passing into elements inside us where we go when others treat us different. Don't shake your head and offer pity over my amputated legs. Ask instead, what, where, why they walked, kicked, dragged, were slumped upon. How a warrior I was born.

Don't nod in understanding without looking straight into my eyes which still sparkle in my guillotined head on the butcher block. How a warrior I was reborn.

Don't put your arms around mine without feeling the compacted air that extends beyond my shredded joints. How a warrior I was born, again and again and again.

Joan of Arc, Takeko, Lozen, Rani of Jhansi, rising, falling, rising. Don't offer to cover me up with your tainted blanket. With your prude coat. With your carefully sculpted sentences pulling a spoof that you are wise. Don't smirk at distances between loves. Don't try walking on my footprint's ashes still smoldering. Don't look for my hands to grip, to tell a joint story. Don't. Don't. Just watch. Just watch as my remaining petals keep disappearing. Watch the air around you solidify. Watch the ground beneath you harden like metamorphic rocks. Watch till I become a whisper at the end of the last drop of water. And then, you can scream.

*Joan of Arc, Nakano Takeko, Lozen, Rani of Jhansi: French, Japanese, Native American, and Indian women warriors respectively

This poem was inspired by the sculpture of Australian artist and poet, Elizabeth 'Lish' Škec.

Of Skulls and Butterflies
Boris Glikman

As a small boy I loved chasing butterflies.

One day, I discovered that the butterfly I had caught had wings which resembled profiles of two human faces; one the mirror image of the other.

When I looked closer, I realised that the wings not only resembled faces, but were indeed faces, shrunken and parched, yet still undeniably real human heads. The butterfly had somehow managed to commandeer these craniums for its own selfish purposes and employ them for flight. Or perhaps the wings either evolved or atrophied from normal butterfly substance into human flesh and skin.

The insect flapped the wings rapidly, trying in desperation to escape my grasp. It seemed to be completely oblivious to the conversation taking place between the two heads, not noticing their fickle expressions of joy, amusement, puzzlement, pleasure which lingered but for an instant and then were gone.

The butterfly kept beating and beating its wings while the two faces continued talking, as if they were just old acquaintances who bumped into each other on the street. Their conversation also reflected this familiarity, comprised as it was of pleasantries and trivialities.

The Be(e)ing of a Tyger
Boris Glikman

PROSE VERSION

The identical coloration of tigers and bees is no random coincidence, without any significance. The real reason for this pun of evolution is actually quite astounding, almost beyond belief.

The simple truth is that the animal that the world knows as a "tiger" has never existed. The true nature of this creature is revealed if you are brave enough to give it a good shake. Once you have done so, you will witness an incredible transformation: the tiger will begin crumbling into pieces until there is nothing left of it, not even a piece of hide, and in its place...thousands upon thousands of bees will appear, as if out of nowhere, buzzing angrily and flying off in all directions.

For you see, a tiger is not a genuine animal. Rather, it is a great collection of Africanised honey bees, also known as killer bees, that have formed themselves into the shape of a tiger. They use this particular configuration to satisfy their great hunger for fresh meat.

All the characteristics of a tiger can be easily explained by this state of affairs: the tiger's roar is really the collective humming of countless bees; the colour of its stripes comes from the hue of bees' bodies; its sharp teeth and claws are, in fact, bees' stingers and its ferocity is due to the notoriously aggressive nature of the killer bees.

Verse Version

Tyger, tyger burning bright
in the forests of the night.
Yet look closer
you will see
all is not what seems to bee.

Bees and tiger
the same colour
a coincidence?
Surely that makes
little sense!

Eeny, meeny, miny, moe
Catch a tiger by the toe.
Shake him hard
and make him hiss.
This reveals
he's made of bees.

Once you stir him
you will find
bees are gone,
naught left behind.

In their hunger for fresh meat,
bees are practicing deceit.
Alas, the tiger we all adore
is but nothing but a roar.

The Final Regret

Boris Glikman

I realise instantly
that fighting against
this creature is futile,
for when I try to
beat off its attacks upon me,
it reveals itself to be
comprised entirely of
a mass of carnivorous worms,
every fibre of its body
assuming the form of
a writhing maggot.

No, this isn't just a
five or six-headed hydra...
this is a billion-headed hydra,
infinitely more powerful than
any super-predator.

And so I lie back,
assuming as comfortable a position
as the situation will allow
and let it devour me...

My last and only twinge of regret
is that I had always secretly hoped
to be eaten alive by a big cat instead.

I recall how
(in my idle hours of daydreaming)

I have often longed to lie naked,
exposed to the elements,
on the soft grass
of African savanna
and feel the lion's
moist, sandpapery tongue
slowly and methodically
lick my skin clean
before ripping me open
with its canines,
gorging upon my innards
and then finally
gnawing on my bones.

And now, alas,
this yearning of mine
shall never be fulfilled...
I sigh...
as my last breath escapes...

Revelata Subterranea
Boris Glikman

One day,
my friends and I descended
into the sewers
beneath the metropolis
and discovered the most unusual eel-like creatures
lounging indolently
on the concrete banks of the subterranean river.

There they were,
lying close to the river's edge,
only deigning to bestir
and dip their heads languidly
into the passing current,
when a particularly choice morsel
of human waste floated by.

Their appearance overpowered me
with its repulsiveness.

"How could Evolution ever
conceive and give birth to such a horrible
abomination?"
I remember wondering to myself,
"How could Nature ever allow
such a glaring insult against Herself
to arise and flourish;
such a travesty,
such a betrayal,
such a perversion of the very natural order?"

Yet when I looked closer
at these anathemas,
a most astounding feature
revealed itself to me.

Somehow, through some playful whim
of the Goddess who directs
and oversees the evolutionary process,
these overgrown worms
developed human faces.

Nay, not just human faces,
but visages of angelic beauty
such that no earthly woman
would ever dare to possess,
lest the Gods become spiteful and jealous.

This discovery was so unexpected,
the radiance of their mien so intense,
I stood transfixed,
unable to take my gaze
even for an instant
away from these heavenly subterrestrial creatures.

Their eyes looked at me
with all the cognition of a person;
Their facial expressions were those
of kindness, serenity, wisdom.

There were two over to the left,
holding their heads close to one another,
gazing deeply, just like two lovers,
into each other's eyes.

Suddenly I felt an odd sort of compassion for them.

A Dog's Tale (Seen Through the Windowpain)
Boris Glikman

Often my dogs lie
at the front door
and stare longingly
at the world
through the windowpane.

They can see clearly
freedom,
sunshine,
wide open spaces
outside.

It seems to be
right within reach,
yet something impenetrable
is in their way,
the nature of which
they cannot comprehend.

The mechanics of door-opening
is a deep mystery to them,
but they display great versatility
in their efforts to solve this dilemma.

Sometimes they jump
up and down,
yapping and wagging their tails,
as if impatience will make the door
open quicker.

At other times they resort
to aggressive tactics,
clawing at the handle
or digging under the sill
to force their way out.

Occasionally
they lie patiently,
having faith
that the door is destined
to swing open
sooner or later.

Now and then they behave
as if there is no door,
having convinced themselves
they are outside already.

Once in a while
they shrink back in fear
when the door *is* unlocked,
so accustomed have they become
to being captive.

Aren't we all like them in a way?

Our noses too are pressed
against the closed door
of illusion and ignorance.

Beyond it we can clearly discern
freedom,
joy,
beauty.

Yet some inexplicable force
keeps the access blocked,
and we can only gaze wistfully
at the richness of life
through the windowpain
of our mind.

Basking in the Morning Sun
Michael Mwangi Macharia

Every morning the village dog
after roaming the whole night
lies on a deserted path;

The lizards and crocs
emerged from the depths lie on hot rocks
to partake of the morning rays
essential for energy and life;

Even the bees are alive
as they buzz on the petals
and suck sweet juices
as butterflies flap wings
in freedom over the meadow;

Humans are too engaged
to sit and savour elements

offered freely by Mother Nature
as they seek to build wealth
often at the cost of poor health.

The Dog Slept
Rhys Hughes

The dog slept
like a log last night.
He is a long sausage dog
so he looked the part apart from
his stubby legs and tail,
but those could have been branches
or twigs, I suppose.

    The log slept
    like a dog last night.
    It is a magical sentient log
    activated by some abstruse spell
    but not a spell from hell,
    so there's no wildfire I should put out
    like an agitated cat.

A Deluxe Duck

Rhys Hughes

I am a deluxe duck,
higher, softer, faster
than any ordinary duck,
and if I was a doctor
I'd be a highly rated
specialist, not a quack.

And if I was a manager
I'd give myself the sack
and make that sack vaster
than any cloth bag sold
openly on the high street.

But webbed are my feet.
I'm just a fine old duck.

Planet of Plants
Rhys Hughes

Planet of plants,
rookery of rocks,
mouthful of rants,
cabinet of socks.

Yet the gibbon swings free
while the panda
sips tea.

Bookcase of faces,
bathtub of smiles,
harp of bootlaces,
waste of old styles.

Still those aardvarks agree
because the yeti
can flee.

Billabong of wrongs,
comets of wordplay,
forked tongue prongs
or ossified gateways.

In all candour the slanders
usually support
pandas.

The Vegetarian
Tony Peak

The person I used to be
Loved how you would taste
Accompanied by sesame,
Whether on the grill, or sauté
With anticipation I would baste
But the person I want to be
Loves to see you free
Not under lock and key
Thriving on land and sea
And your life not gone to waste

Deconstruction
Tony Peak

Hydrogen into Helium started the fusion
That allowed Carbon and Oxygen
Together in measured collusion
With Phosphorus, Sulfur and Nitrogen
To create a stupendous profusion
Of a will stronger than Tungsten
And a love immune to erosion
That engendered this hallucinogen
We call human triumph and delusion

Bacteria
Teika Marija Smits

As a schoolgirl,
I found it easy enough to remember
the differences between plant and animal cells.
The former contained large, watery vacuoles,
sturdy walls of cellulose
and chloroplasts that glowed green.

The latter had none of these things.

But bacteria, or prokaryotes
(the *pro*logue to eukaryotes),
were strange little beasts
that had features of both
kinds of cells.
They evaded easy definition.

Years later, as a mother to a schoolboy,
and on homework duty,
I had to Google the features of bacteria.
And there they were, the hairy little beggars,
with their flailing flagella, their cell walls not of
        cellulose,
their free-floating DNA.

Thanks to my childhood science lessons,
I only ever thought of bacteria as "baddies"
but now I know that they're necessary
for our bodies and the planet.
Perhaps they could do
with some better branding?

Exclamation Fish
Teika Marija Smits

Always, there is a look of surprise
when my secret identity is discovered.

So, you're a writer! my neighbour exclaims.
What sort of books do you write?
My wife loves a good crime, she does.
She's big on those 1930s detectives, you know. Me,
I'm more of a manuals man.
Practical-like.

What do I say to that?!
I imagine penning a handy guide
to the detectives of the 1930s,
trilby-hatted, moustachioed,
dropping in snippets of advice
on how to fix a corrupt carburettor,
how to wallpaper round a tricky corner;
both husband and wife now avid readers of my work.

Instead I smile, say, *What do I write?*
Oh, this and that. Poems, stories.
Nothing you'd have heard of.

We swim away from this murky topic,
into the familiar, clear shallows of small talk.
In time, drifting back to ourselves,
the comfort of our own ponds.

Laika's Prayer
Teika Marija Smits

Our Laika,
our Comrade,
who dwells in the heavens above,
provide us each day
with our daily bone,
fresh air,
green fields,
a loving home.
And keep us safe
from those who wish us ill;
from those with no room in their hearts for dogs.
Our Laika, our Sister,
forever numinous,
remember us always.
So be it, Dog.

Rubies
Teika Marija Smits

Ripe tomatoes, warm
to the touch. The jewels of late
summer, earthy-sweet.

Cat, Caught
Rebecca Bellamy

Black and white fluffball
sat in a smelly mint bush;
green-tongued and guilty.

Friends
Peter Banks

Diamonds are a girl's best friend
Apparently
And dogs are a man's best friend
I'm sure you will agree
So why oh why did Bowie cry
Beware of Diamond Dogs ?
He said 'Diamond dogs are poachers
And they hide behind trees
Hunt you to the ground they will
Mannequins with kill appeal'
It doesn't sound too friendly
To me.

Toad
Richard Temple

The toad squats -
dead eyes darting, delirious.
Spittle slicks his hideous jowl -
panting painfully -
gaping, gasping.
A buckled leg hangs, swelling, limp.
Chin to bloated belly.
Quivering, juddering,
his withered hand covering
the paper cup - slip, drip,
as he struggles to sip.
Worrying, muttering - smothering memories,
cradling cold cappuccino.

Fabricant
Tony Peak

the blue robot cries
a dynamic universe
in static metal

Global Worming
Richard Temple

Whispers of worms on the wind
exhale:
winding and weaving warnings.

Throbbing, pulsating, decomposing -
the whole world rotting.
Glutenous guts groan with gastric gasses,
and defecate mountainous moist mulch,
composting, dissolving, foetid and fermenting.

A global necropolis hisses,
dismisses decaying dermal crust.
Inexorable consumption,
vermicular digestion:
a graveyard gastronomy.
Grim mastication gives birth
to flickering, flailing life,

and the whisper of worms on the wind
exhale:
belching.

I Am a Kangaroo
Rhys Hughes

I am a kangaroo.
What's it to you?
I jump around the page.
but I'm not enraged.
Sure, you might
be hopping mad
or flopping from
the core exhaustion
following exasperation.
You might even be
gadfly-bewinged
but that's your lookout.
I'm not stopping you
being furious or sad.
Be whatever you wish,
a fish like a trout
or barracuda
with a snout,
hefty pike or minnow,
lefty perch or manta ray,
sodden and diluvial.
Why should I care?
I am satisfied and glad
just to be a marsupial.

The Mule
Rhys Hughes

The mule must be a fool
because he lost his tool,
a very expensive slide rule,
in a large bowl of gruel
and now he can't find it.
I have questions to ask.

      Hold on! The mule knows
      how to use a slide rule?
      Then he's certainly no fool
      and you must be a ghoul
      to make that suggestion.
      No question about it.

The Lion Doesn't
Rhys Hughes

      The lion doesn't
      like eating tomatoes
      unless they are
      ROAR!!!!!

The Cat and the Whale
Santosh Bakaya

The Blue Whale was pretty lazy, everyone knew.
Because of its slothful ways, friends it had few.
A cute cat eyed it with undisguised feline curiosity.
But the whale was not known for its amiability.

The cat grinned and resiliently wagged its fluffy tail.
Extending a friendly paw; its actions to no avail.
"Not interested," The whale's expressions loudly said.
The cat pleaded, coerced and cajoled, eyes very red.

The whale rudely shunned the cat's friendly ventures,
plainly unwilling to embark with it on any adventures.
The wicked whale whacked it. What a misadventure!
The poor cat is now moving around with cat dentures!

Tuffy and Muffy
Santosh Bakaya

Tuffy, the bat was somersaulting and making clicking
    sounds.
Muffy, the owl was hooting incessantly on its nocturnal
    rounds.
They saw a huge rhinoceros lumbering towards a water-
    hole.
This weird scene on their fragile bodies took a very
    heavy toll.

As the scene unfolded before him, Tuffy loudly
    chuckled.
Muffy watched, lips pursed, with curiosity white-
    knuckled.
Behind the bushes, quickly a scared squirrel scampered.
In a syrupy voice, whispered the rhino, highly
    pampered.

"What pranks are you up to? I am the king of the
    jungle."
I will kick you two out of the jungle, if you try to
    bungle."
"Rhino dear, please get a reality check, you are
    confused.
The lion is supposedly, the king, and we are not
    amused."

Said the two buddies in one voice to the rhinoceros
    bloated.

"You are the ones confused, I AM the king," the rhino
gloated.
He trumpeted so loudly, that every leaf on every tree
shook.
"You can boast on, we care two hoots, you oaf! You
crook!"

They saw something slithering through the
undergrowth.
"Is it a snake or a mongoose?" Highly scared, gasped
both.
"It is only a piece of twig, moving with the breeze, bro.
Don't be such a coward, look there comes the canny
crow."

Soon, the bat, the owl and the crow broke into a
maladroit jig.
The rhino watched, as the jig slowly turning into a big
gig.
Soon every animal of the jungle jumped onto the band
wagon.
Forgetting his kingly ambitions, the rhino also joined
the fun.

A Found Poem from 1985
Don Webb

"It's like love. It's exactly like looking for love."
She dressed like a hippy from two decades before.
She was squelching through the marshy field near our
    cabin.
The water was rust brown from its iron content.
Cattle grazed there when it wasn't too wet.
I asked her, "What is like love?"
You may attribute that to my poetic soul,
Or my belief that hippy chicks are easy
Or both.
"THAT!"
She pointed to a large cow patty
Where a ring of *pilocybe semilanceata* had sprouted
Brown and slimy with dark brown nipples on the top of
    their crowns
"It's like love!"

Fluorite

Don Webb

The crystal structure of fluorite,
That is to say calcium fluoride,
Is like most halides
Shaped like two four sided pyramids
Grew base to base.
It can be milky, green, brown or (in this case) purple
In daylight
In UV it glows crazy green
In the context of archeology, gemmology, classical
studies, and Egyptology,
the Latin terms *murrina* and *myrrhina* refer to fluorite.
At the rock store in 1993
Fifty cents a crystal
At the Wiccan store
Thirteen bucks each.

Mineral Poem

Richard Temple

Tridymite,
Sard Torite
an ode to Iron
Ore stalagmites

Two Birds

Anna Tambour

Two birds in two cages
side by side.
They've got seed. They've got water.
Their cages are floored with paper.
Each can sit on a perch—
a dowel as clean as a tree stripped to
      toothpicks.

Their homes are clean as two platters
washed and ready,
always ready.

Their owner's perch is a stool
in this market.
Her home, her work—all a busy clutter.
A world away from the kondo neatness
of the homes of her two birds.

Two birds born to languages so far apart,
      they might not have heard each other
      as birds
if they hadn't seen each other
and smelled each other's feathers, mites, and
      skin, every day,
so close, just too far away to hurt each other.

They can see each other, but sing?
Their owner can hardly hear a thing out of
      them

over the torrent of people buying, deciding,
        trying, greeting, motoring and
        shuffling past.

Two birds in two cages
side by side.
They've got seed. They've got water.
Each can sit on a perch
and babble at the other.

Two birds in two cages
a world away from the torrent
on the other side of their bars.

That's How I Go
Rhys Hughes

I chained my dog
to the end of my nose
and chained my cat
to the end of my toe
and that's how I go.

Pulled along by my pets
much to the dismay
of the local vets
but my dog is a wolf
and my cat is a tiger
and that's how I went.

Rock of Ages
Rhys Hughes

What was the Rock of Ages:
igneous, metamorphic or sedimentary?
The question isn't elementary
even for geologists.

It depends on the duration of the Ages,
in much the same way
that the length of a book
is controlled by the number of its pages.

Actually that's not quite true.
A million-page book might have text
printed in a font of such massive size
that it's a relatively rapid read.

So the Rock of Ages could even be
just a stone of seconds
skimmed across the waters of Time
like a flattened pebble.

But I think it was probably a big chunk
of flint, in other words
a cryptocrystalline form of quartz
with glints in the tilted
tints of its silted sunken meaning.

Pomelo

Beni Sumer Yanthan

April, and the back of my father's garden has
welcomed the last pomelos for the year.
Every year they reappear like the collected poems
Of a poet writing his absinthe-clad emotions
With the furore of a stained tongue –
On a piece of parchment paper half eaten by termites.

No one knew who had fastened the tree there –
At the back – next to the lime tree whose leaves
Droop in obligatory succession whenever it is time
For the fruiting.
They sprout every year, heavy as a poem
That only birds can home.

In the winter, they are sweet and somewhat sour,
Splitting your tongue into a maze of tastes
That prickles your nostalgia and usurps your saliva,
And then slowly, as the new moon neuters the earth,
The pomelo, fruiting and fattened on earth for so long,
Turns murderously bitter until the first wind of a new
       winter

 And so it is now April's end, and the pomelo's first
       bitter flesh
Is about to meet tongue.

Inside the house, mother has had her fill of tea and
       sons,

and is scouring the house for something to write home
about.
Father is in his fourth dream, where he is meeting his
old friends
for a session of blackjack, under an oft-forgotten
pomelo tree.

Their cats lie idly by the TV, smeared with the stench
of an April air thick with flamboyant breaths.
The daughter sits writing on her table where her tongue
has just met
The bitter knock of a knuckled pomelo
And has had her tongue rendered tight.

Mango Pulp Fiction
Maithreyi Karnoor

Like vanquished kings and squished nothings
The alphonsos, here, have no show
Without the ring of the hype and bling
Sweetly loved the mancurads grow

Here pulp fiction has got its own diction
Old uncle Albuquerque barbed in his garb
When comes in for a juicy benediction
Is redeemed as silly Albukar baab.

144

Animal, Vegetable, Mineral
Maithreyi Karnoor

'Tara' I call you out of my visceral compulsion to name
       everything
animal, vegetable, mineral
(the purple wildflowers
on the path to the spot from where I speak with my
       lover
are 'Mehrunnisa';
my mother's gold *gajra* handed down to her by her
       grandmother
is 'Sundara Bai').
You are a rhesus monkey
and I, a flunkey of machinations – my own and others'
       – that say
land is owned
as are tubes of toothpaste, and bottles of facewash
       liquid,
and sandal-scented soaps.
I like to think they cleanse me and make me smell nice
before I present myself to be looked at and felt.
It is not food as you discovered
after biting, breaking
and flinging it about the land – my land – in frustration:
what doesn't nourish is useless to you.
Your breasts don't sag. You haven't had babies. Neither
       have I.
I think that's a good thing but you may not agree.
That must be the human-animal conflict they speak of.
I bought a new facewash. It's honey-gel.

It's more expensive than the last one which was neem-
extract.
I'm not letting you get your tiny hands on this one.

Penguins
Mitali Chakravarty

Penguins waddle
black and white on the
snows of the Antarctic.

They never made it to the
Arctic — could not survive
the heat of the tropics!

White melts slowly to
shades of blue and dark,
no longer absolute, stark.

No longer are the tints sharp.
Will the penguin continue with
hues that do not meet?

Will they survive the expanding seas
with their extremes of black and white?
Or will they alter with the changing tides?

Zircon
David Rix

I have never held in my hands
such an ancient storyteller
Part of me, of course, yearns to,
but maybe such tellers of tales deserve silk gloves
clean rooms, robotic arms
sealed cabernets, museum-grade bullet-proof glass
or at least a comfy chair in peace
there to sip mellow wine
and remember
the old days
and nursing your inclusions
from 4.4 billion years of rains

Red Flint
David Rix

The romance of a stone
"Here, human being, I have a gift for you."
The shiny thorns of hope, the token
And languages that words have never heard of
"It's just a red flint that I found
And polished, and thought of you."

Dug out of a London ditch
Under the greasy food carton, the bike tyre
The bedraggled water-bones of the city
Where furtive wanderers do not linger
Sewage stink and brine and oil
The mud wiped away in dull incarnadine

What language do you want to hear?
"Oh how pretty, and what a lovely colour, thank you."
There are many in the stones and all based in mud
If you speak the frozen lies of diamonds
Then it is good if it's just a pretty rock
If you cannot hear this flint's whispers

Ground smooth with grit and ruined clothes
Polished and buffed, this pebble of home
Flesh-red depths to sink through in dreams
Of threads connecting people like
A stone-deep transcontinental railway
This remains, to me, the greater treasure

So many languages
And inversions of languages
"Here – take this red flint
That I polished for you
Place it among your diamonds
And remember me when I'm gone."

Pseudomorph

David Rix

Imagining from this point
Our own world set in stone
Unearthed in future mud and dust
By weary students of anthropalaeontology
If there are still those to give such a name

"Pseudomorphs, you know. A vanished substance
replaced by uncaring stone or crystal
'bout anything can fossilise, dear sir
though I'm sure I don't need to tell you that
one so erudite and wise as yourself."

So how long do we have to wait
For our discarded shoes and aglets
Or mobile phones and stray detritus
To grace a museum's shelves in stone or gem
Dusty traces or shimmering with crystal light?

"You've seen the precious ones, right?
Opal seashells? Emerald snails? Coral replaced by
        agate?
Or gem-bone turned into earrings and bling?
Pseudomorphs rule the world, dear sir.
The phantasms, the storytellers."

Answer: there are already human fossils
Pseudomorphs of calcite, or gypsum, or mud
Those stones that grow fast like fireworks
But for gems, we'll have to wait

For agate children's toys or stray bolts replaced by
fire opal

"The rarest of the rare, dear sir
The pseudomorphs to rule them all
Wonders from a bygone age
The ancient artefact, the colours of the rainbow
Shimmering with light and fire"

And I have a new goal for humanity now
To keep going, to grow and to survive
Long enough for there to be
Illicit trade among the collectors and rockhounds
in opal earbuds or disposable cups of emerald

"See this? Museum grade. As I'm sure you can see.
Exceptional and unique – though for one like yourself
I hardly need to point that out – and dear sir …
I need it gone. So … special deal? Tonight only?
Finest opal pseudomorph after gym shoe I ever saw …"

Three Limericks
Mitali Chakravarty

LADYBUG

Ladybug, ladybug red and gold,
Why do you sit on my sofa, so bold?
You look like a toy or a brooch,
Absolutely unrelated to the cockroach.
Yet, you are of the same family, I am told!

PARROTS

Parrots in a flock fly high
In the uninterrupted blue sky.
But when they stay low,
A-squawking they go —
Noisy, chattering, without batting an eye!

CRICKETS

Oh cricket, Oh cricket, Oh crickets!
Not the one we play with wickets—
But the green ones that sat
At the Great Wall on my lap,
How could you all fly in without tickets?

Something to Mention

Rhys Hughes

It is my contention
that if I was a cat
instead of a writer
my future would be
considerably brighter
and I would receive
a lot more attention
than I currently do.

(The same goes for you.)

We are all animals (some of us are birds) and all animals are equal but some animals are more equal (those who are birds are more eagle) than others. Blow me down
              with a feather.

We are all plants, especially when we stand in pants.

Many of us are rocks, stony faced and/or reliable. Friable,
              inviolable
              classifiable
              justifiable, not pliable,
                 and that's undeniable
in the gleaming geology of our
              molten souls.

BIOGRAPHICAL NOTES

ANDREW J. WILSON lives in Edinburgh, Scotland. His short stories, non-fiction and poetry have appeared all over the world. Recent publications include poems in *Star*Line, Eye to the Telescope, Summer Anywhere (Dreich), Gallus: Poetry Scotland's Sassy Sibling* and *Wuxing Lyrical: Playful Poems Based on Chinese Astrology* (Gloomy Seahorse Press). He was nominated for the Science Fiction Poetry Association's Dwarf Stars Award in 2020 and 2022.

ANDREW HOOK has had numerous stories and books published since 1994 but not so much poetry. His contribution offers an explanation as to why.

SANTOSH BAKAYA. Internationally acclaimed for her poetic biography of Mahatma Gandhi, Ballad of Bapu, Santosh Bakaya, Ph.D, is an award-winning poet, novelist, TEDx speaker, biographer, with 23 books published across different genres.

REBA PATNAIK is from Odisha, India, and says, "Professionally I am a teacher. From teaching to penning short stories and poems… Where did the twist and turn take place, I just don't remember. Honestly saying, teaching is my passion and writing is my inspiration. My venting lets me experience living life every moment with love, grace and gratitude."

MITALI CHAKRAVARTY writes for peace, love and harmony and in that spirit founded Borderless Journal, which has just brought out its first anthology, *Monalisa No Longer Smiles: An Anthology of Writings from Across the World.*

SAMANTHA UNDERHILL is a poet, voice artist, educator, researcher, mother, and lover of all things dark but beautiful. Born in Appalachia, Samantha's connection to haunting, soul-touching scenery, music, and folklore, gives her a unique connection to deep meaningful melancholy. Samantha is influenced by writers of dark storytelling poetry and literature, such as H.P. Lovecraft, Edgar Allan Poe, and Jorge Luis Borges.

ROMAN GODZICH is a polyglot who has lived and worked in several countries. He has worked in e-commerce, travel, online gaming, and professional training among other industries, and has designed search engines, advertising platforms, and online booking engines. He currently manages content and user experience for an online travel company. He is the author of the science fiction thriller *No Higher Ground.* Roman grew up in Manhattan and now makes his home in Connecticut. When not working or writing, Roman enjoys deep-sea fishing, reading, and gourmet cooking.

BOB LOCK was born on the Gower Peninsula, Wales, back in the Dark Ages when there were no computers, televisions or FTL spaceships. (Ok, there still aren't any FTLs whilst writing this, but who knows how long this bio might be around?). First published in *Cold Cuts 1 & 2* (Horror anthos). Debut Dark Fantasy novel *Flames of Herakleitos* published in March 2007. His Urban Fantasy Novel *The Empathy Effect* (set in Swansea) published in September 2010. Many other shorts in anthologies and webzines since then.

ANNA TAMBOUR'S latest book is the 2023 collection published by Oddness, *Death Goes to the Dogs*.

SUCHITA PARIKH-MUNDUL is a writer and copy editor. Her articles have appeared in magazines like *Femina* and *The Swaddle*. Her poetry can be read in *The Bombay Literary Magazine, Gulmohur Quarterly, Narrow Road, Outlook India, Muse India,* Sahitya Akademi's *Indian Literature*, and other journals. Her work has also been included in anthologies such as *Amity: peace poems, The Well-Earned* (both Hawakal, 2022), *On Hunger: A Poetrygram Anthology* (ed. Helen Cox, 2023), other international compilations, and *The Yearbook of Indian Poetry in English 2022-2023* (forthcoming, Hawakal).

TIM NEWTON ANDERSON is a former journalist and PR manager who started writing a few years ago. He has had a couple of dozen stories published in a wide variety of magazines and anthologies including some by *Black Scat* and *Emanations* but this is his first attempt at poetry.

MAITHREYI KARNOOR is a novelist, short story writer, poet and translator from the Indian state of Karnataka. Her first novel, *Sylvia: Distant Avuncular Ends* was published first by Westland in India and then by Neem Tree Press in the UK. She was awarded a Charles Wallace Fellowship in 2022. She is currently working on a new novel and several poetry collections.

BENI SUMER YANTHAN is an indigenous, tribal poet from Nagaland, India belonging to the Lotha tribe. She works in the capacity of Assistant Professor at Nagaland University, Kohima Campus. She also writes essays and commentaries on various socio-political-cultural aspects of Nagaland.

DOUG SKINNER has contributed to *Cabinet, Weirdo, The Fortean Times,* and other fine periodicals. His books include fiction, cartoons, and many translations; his music is available on Bandcamp. He has written music for numerous shows, most conspicuously for Bill Irwin's award-winning *Regard of Flight.*

155

MICHAEL MWANGI MACHARIA is a poet from Nakuru Kenya. He attended Moi University where he studied English and Literature. He has written many verses and published literary articles in newspapers. He is inspired by beautiful and varied environments. He writes to understand his thoughts and feelings. He is also an associate editor with Striidas Publishers as well as founder of the Modern African Poetry Group. He uses poetry to promote education and nurture youthful talent.

DON WEBB has written professionally since 1986 with 25 books and over 400 articles, stories and poems. He teaches horror writing at UCLA Extension, shot fireworks professionally for a decade and is an expert on the Greek Magical Papyri.

MARIE C LECRIVAIN curates *Dashboard Horus: A Bird's Eye of the Universe.* Her writing has appeared in *Bottle Rockets, Nonbinary Review, Orbis,* and *Pirene's Fountain.* She's the editor of *Ashes to Stardust: A David Bowie Tribute Anthology.*

TONY PEAK is an Active Member of SFWA, and an Associate Member of the HWA. He is represented by Ethan Ellenberg of the Ethan Ellenberg Literary Agency. His interests include progressive thinking, futurism, and planetary exploration. Residing in southwest Virginia, he has a wonderful view of New River.

JOJI MATHEW, (perhaps known in small groups under the neutral pseudonym of 'writingwaters') was born in 1964, brought up, and educated in Kerala; joined as a Lecturer in English in Shillong, then continued teaching at a paramedical college in Saudi Arabia, and went on working later as Regulatory Officer at Servier, a French Pharmaceutical company. Currently lives in Assam. Deeply involved in the beautiful evolution of thought and consciousness. A vegetarian by practice, intensely interested in Eastern Mysticism.

VANDANA KUMAR is a French teacher, translator, recruitment consultant, Indie Film Producer, cinephile and poet in New Delhi, India. Her poems have been published in national and international websites of repute like *Mad Swirl, Grey Sparrow Journal, The Piker Press, Dissident Voice, Borderless Journal, Madras Courier, Outlook* etc. She has featured in literary journals like *Fine Lines* and anthologies like *Harbinger Asylum, Kali Project, But You Don't Look Sick* etc. Her cinema articles appear regularly in *Just-Cinema* and *Daily Eye.* Her debut collection of poems *Mannequin Of Our Times* was published in February 2023. The book has been awarded The Panorama International Book Award 2023.

VICTORIA DAY has had several supernatural short stories published by *Nebula Press, The Silent Companions, The Ghastling, Supernatural Tales, Vault of Evil, Sarob, Hypnogoria, TK Pulp, Side Real Press* and *Ghost and Scholars*. In 2021 her novella, *Greven Hall* came third in The Ghastling's novella competition. Her play *Take What You Want* was performed in 2022 at The Nidderdale One Act play Festival. She lives in Harrogate, North Yorkshire with her family and the subject of her poem and his brother, two border terriers.

MIA TIJAM is acknowledged as one of the editors who have advanced Philippine Speculative Fiction and its writers, co-editing with Charles S. Tan the *Philippine Speculative Fiction Sampler*. She also served as Editor for the Special Section for PWDs and PADs of the Cultural Center of the Philippines Literary Journal, ANI 41: *Paglalakbay: Lakad, Layag, Lipad*; and Guest Editor in *Philippine Genre Stories*. Her work had been published in *Philippines Free Press, Expanded Horizons, Bewildering Stories*; and anthologies like *The Farthest Shore: Fantasy Fiction from the Philippines, BRAVURA: An Anthology of 21st Century Philippine Fiction*, and *In Certain Seasons: Mothers Write in the Time of COVID*. Her debut short fiction collection *Flowers for Thursday* was a Finalist in the 40th Philippine National Book Awards.

TEIKA MARIJA SMITS is a UK-based writer and freelance editor. Her debut poetry pamphlet, *Russian Doll*, was published by Indigo Dreams Publishing in 2021. A fan of all things fae, she is delighted by the fact that Teika means fairy tale in Latvian.

REBECCA BELLAMY is a secondary schoolgirl who, amidst masses of homework, has many hobbies, from poetry and art to sewing and sculpting, and she enjoys all creative tasks.

BORIS GLIKMAN is a writer, poet and philosopher from Melbourne, Australia. He says: "Writing for me is a spiritual activity of the highest degree. Writing gives me the conduit to a world that is unreachable by any other means, a world that is populated by Eternal Truths, Ineffable Questions and Infinite Beauty. It is my hope that these stories of mine will allow the reader to also catch a glimpse of this universe." Two of his pieces in this collection, 'Octoworld' and 'The Unbearable Light-ness of Shadow', were originally published in the anthology, *I Used to be an Animal Lover: an extraordinary and eclectic collection of short stories*.

ANITA NAHAL, Ph.D., CDP, is a Pushcart Prize-nominated Indian American writer and academic. She has four books of poetry, one of flash fiction, four for children, and five edited anthologies to her credit. Her third poetry book, *What's Wrong with us Kali Women?* (Kelsay, 2021) was nominated by Cyril Dabydeen, Guyanese Indian Canadian poet, and novelist, as the best poetry book 2021 for *Ars Notoria*. It's also a compulsory reading in an elective course on Multicultural Society, Utrecht University, the Netherlands. Her latest poetry book is a collection of ekphrastic poetry, *Kisses at the Espresso Bar* (Kelsay, 2022). Anita's poems have appeared in numerous journals in the US, UK, Asia, and Australia and have been anthologized in many collections, including *The Polaris Trilogy*, which will be sent to the moon in the Space X launch. Anita's first novel, *Drenched Thoughts* is due for release this year. Nahal teaches at the University of the District of Columbia, Washington DC. She is the daughter of Sahitya Akademi award-winning Indian novelist and professor, Late Dr. Chaman Nahal, and her mother, Late Dr. Sudarshna Nahal was also an educationist and principal of a K-12 school. Originally from New Delhi, India, Anita resides in the US. Her family includes her son, daughter-in-law, and a golden doodle.

PETER BANKS has had many jobs, from psychiatric nurse to homoeopath to donkey man giving rides on the beach. Many interests as well. But the consuming passion in life has been the written word, reading them and sometimes writing them.

CARMELO RAFALA'S stories have appeared in various anthologies, such as *American Short Stories Volume VII, Stories for Chip: A Tribute to Samuel R Delany, American Monsters, Part Two*, and others. His novella, *The Madness of Pursuit*, is published by Guardbridge Books. He lives on the south coast of the UK, with too many books and not enough Scotch.

FABIO FERNANDES is a Brazilian writer currently based in São Paulo. He has published several books, among which the novels *Os Dias da Peste, Back in the USSR*, and *Love Will Tear Us Apart* (in Portuguese) and the novella *Under Pressure* and the collection *Love: An Archaeology* (in English). Also a translator, he is responsible for the translation to Brazilian Portuguese of several SF novels, including *Neuromancer* and *A Clockwork Orange*. His short stories have been published online in Brazil, Portugal, Romania, the UK, New Zealand, and USA, and also in *Steampunk II: Steampunk Reloaded, The Apex Book of World SF, Vol 2, Stories for Chip*. Co-edited (with Djibril al-Ayad) the postcon anthology *We See a Different Frontier*, and, with Francesco Verso, the anthology *Solarpunk - Come ho imparato ad amare il futuro*. Graduate of Clarion West, class of 2013. Formerly reviewer for *The Fix, SF Signal, Tor.com*, and slush reader for *Clarkesworld Magazine*.

JEANNE VAN BUREN is best known for her anthology, *In The Field Of Fire*, with Jack Dann. (Published by TOR). It was a finalist for the 1988 World Fantasy Awards. Her story 'The Apotheosis of Isaac Rosen', with Jack Dann was chosen for *The Years Best Fantasy Stories*, an anthology edited by Art Saha. This story first appeared in *Omni Magazine*. Jeanne also has been acknowledged as a "regional favourite" for her visual art which she has won regional and national awards. She resides in upstate New York.

DAVID RIX is an author, artist and book designer from London's East End, where he has been running the small specialist publisher Eibonvale Press for over fifteen years. His own published books include the novelettes *A Suite in Four Windows* and *Brown is the New Black*, the novella/story collection *Feather* and the novel *A Blast of Hunters*. His first published poetry was in the book *Wuxing Lyrical*, also edited by Rhys Hughes.

REBECCA LOWE is a poet in Swansea, Wales, UK, where it rains cats and dogs almost every day. Her most recent publications are *Blood and Water* (The Seventh Quarry, 2020) and *Our Father Eclipse* (Culture Matters, 2021).

RYHOR CISIECKI is an independent film and theater director, photographer and writer. Now he lives with his wife Volga Grusha and two young sons in a small Belarusian town called Zaslavl.

VOLGA GRUSHA is an actress, poet and hospital clown. With her husband Ryhor Cisiecki and two sons, she lives in a small Belarusian town called Zaslavl.

KUMAR BHATT retired as a Professor of Physics in 2002 at age 69. He says "I received my PhD from the University of Chicago in '62. I have spent twenty-six years of my life in US, the rest of the years in Gujarat, India. After retirement I chose to learn writing. I write whatever occurs to me. Since it is a gift I do not to correct or polish what I write. My daughter Smita, retired last year as a Speech Pathologist from a school system in Georgia, USA. My son Vishwesh Bhatt is a well-known chef in US."

RICHARD TEMPLE is a poet and writer living in Llandeilo, Wales. His poetry has been published in various anthologies, including *They Want All Our Teeth To Be Theirs* (Culture Matters, 2021), *Songs of Peace* (Author's Press, 2022), *Wuxing Lyrical* (Gloomy Seahorse Press, 2022), and *Tranquillity* (Galleon Publishing, 2023), as well as literary journals in Denmark and the USA. His Haikus have featured in the Japanese haiku journal *Paradise*. A reading of his poem 'Atman', accompanied by music he composed, performed, and recorded himself, was included in the *Poetic Phonotheque* project permanent collection at Red Door Gallery in Copenhagen, and he contributed to the *Poetry of Places* online collection. He has been featured and interviewed on the *Fertile Brains* channel in India, and his poem 'Neuroverse' is cited as the inspiration on the sleeve of Papi Di4bL0's 2022 collection *Naked Rainbows in the Dark (Vol. 1)*. Richard is a regular live performer at Cerddi yn Cwrw in Carmarthen, and Poets and Peasants in Lampeter, Wales. He was a semifinalist at the 2021 Swansea Fringe Festival Poetry Slam and reads regularly at spoken word events in Wales and online. He performed on the Monkey Poet stage at the 2022 Unorthodox Paradox Festival in Anglesey, Wales, and is billed to perform again at this year's festival at Wormlow Tump in Herefordshire, England. He co-presented the Metaphor & Melody/Trosiad ac Alaw 'writing for performance' workshop at Llandeilo Literary Festival 2023, has interactive poetry displays included in the forthcoming *Art Soup* exhibition at Lampeter University Library and will be performing at the launch event in May 2023.

PAUL BATTENBOUGH was born in Clydach, Swansea, Wales. He is an artist, musician, composer, writer and occasional poet

JIM MATTHEWS is the author of *Fighting Monsters* (Mirror Books), a memoir of his time spent fighting against *Daesh* (ISIS) in northern Syria. He was charged with terrorism on return to the UK, but charges were finally dropped. He has a degree in Philosophy and Literature and has published short stories in several literary magazines and anthologies.

VIOLETA MARQUEZ was born in Mexico and immigrated to the United States at 18 years old. She is naturalized as American citizen, so she has two nationalities, her career is in accounting and administration, Violeta began to write when she was 16 years old, but she thought her writing was worthless and stopped writing; she returned to her writing at the age of 36- and at 43-years old, Violeta began to share her writing in social media after of the death of her first son. Her writing is to heal the soul.

Printed in Great Britain
by Amazon

38591575R00091